DATE DUE

Oct 31 8			
MAR 21 1988			
	45230		Printed in USA

Techniques of Scenario Planning

Techniques of
Scenario Planning

John Chandler
and Paul Cockle

McGRAW-HILL Book Company (UK) Limited

London · New York · St Louis · San Francisco · Auckland · Bogotá
Guatemala · Hamburg · Johannesburg · Lisbon · Madrid · Mexico
Montreal · New Delhi · Panama · Paris · San Juan · São Paulo
Singapore · Sydney · Tokyo · Toronto

Published by
McGRAW-HILL Book Company (UK) Limited
MAIDENHEAD · BERKSHIRE · ENGLAND

British Library Cataloguing in Publication Data
Chandler, John
   Techniques of Scenario Planning.
   1. Corporate planning
   I. Title   II. Cockle, Paul
   658.4'01   HD30.28
   ISBN 0–07–084570–0

Library of Congress Cataloging in Publication Data
Chandler, John.
   Techniques of Scenario Planning.

   Includes index.
   1. Corporate planning.   I. Cockle, Paul.
II. Title.
HD30.28.C46   658.4'012   81–8346
ISBN 0–07–084570–0   AACR2

12345 AP 8432

Printed and bound in Great Britain by the Alden Press, Oxford

Contents

1.
The system in outline

Duplicate worlds

Ancient philosphers used to argue that duplicate worlds were necessary for assessing the consequences and hence the merits of alternative courses of action. It was said that only by observing the courses of events unfolding in each world could it ever be possible to make valid comparisons between the alternatives and to select the most desirable. Even the early thinkers perceived that society was too complex to project confidently the consequences of competing proposals. Since it was accepted that such duplicate worlds could not exist, they concluded that it was impossible to forecast how humans would arrange their lives under differing circumstances: social behaviour could not be foretold, or the course of society predicted. Doubtless, some felt relieved that mankind, making mess enough of the existing world, did not have others to practise upon. Even so, the notion of a duplicate world, in which social experiments could be carried out, had, and still has, vast appeal. Would it not be intriguing to play all sorts of 'what-if' games without being obliged to suffer the consequences? The timid might grow bold with the experience and the cavalier, cautious.

How have we developed since then? Have we, in our present world, managed to discover some parallel planet to serve our purpose? The answer is, of course 'yes'—but not in the physical way envisaged by the ancients. Two major, and not entirely new, developments have combined to transform the dreams of the ancients into reality. First, modern scientific method, applied to the social sciences, has advanced the use of modelling techniques dramatically. The models of the social sciences are no more than a set of crisply stated hypotheses on the behaviour of well defined groups and individuals, in an equally well defined context. Scientific method is then applied to testing these against available data and rejecting those that are invalid.

Second, the computer has played an enormous part in opening up vast new opportunities in organizing and manipulating data. Intuition is now replaced or supplemented by programs that can examine a multiplicity of data and relationships with which, for reasons of both volume and complexity, the human brain could not grapple unaided. The use of a computer is analogous to a microscope to enable insights into the structure of the systems under examination. Effective factor analysis then moves us toward the ability to build a duplicate of such structures for ourselves.

Two practical examples indicate the currently wide spectrum of research using computers to cope with the vast amount of detail. A Cambridge

1

(England) group has compiled a data base of all recorded information such as church registers, court rolls, and so on for the village of Earl's Colne in Essex from 1380 to 1750.[1] Research into the mobility of agricultural workers and land tenure is no longer subject to the imprecision of terms like 'peasant' and 'serfdom' with automatic assumptions of a 'semi-mystical attachment to the land' and unbreakable local ties. As a result, the validity of representing Continental European (and even Eastern) agrarian societies as adequate patterns of medieval English village life is at least under question.

The second example is the PIMS data base produced by the Strategic Planning Institute of Cambridge, Massachusetts.[2] Research into the underlying characteristics that make some businesses potentially more profitable than others has been fruitful. Profit seems to be correlated with a number of factors, such as market share, growth, vertical intergration, and so on. In assessing corporate strategies, therefore, the way is open to substituting information for hunch, and general labels such as 'packaging' or 'pharmaceuticals', which assume without specifying certain business structures, are replaced with detailed profiles of businesses from which may be generated the likely future contribution to corporate profit.

Duplicate 'worlds' may, therefore, be created and used as test-beds for our understanding of the structure and dynamics of our own. We call such duplicates 'models', rather than 'worlds', because they are normally limited to the small corner of the universe with which we are grappling—as in the two examples quoted above.

The nature of models

The term 'model', however, often releases all sorts of emotional outbursts about machines replacing men and the human condition being reduced to a quadratic equation. It is worth defining the concept. Most people are familiar with model aircraft, trains, or cars, which are no more than scaled-down versions of the real item. Such models may be highly accurate in every detail; others, such as dolls, are much simpler, and the basics alone evoke the reality in our minds.

Physical limitations prevent modelling with complete accuracy in every case. Is this critical? The answer depends on the objective of the analyst in building the model. If he is going to be selective about the characteristics that he imports into the model, his selection must relate to his purpose. Maps are a good example of this principle. If a traveller wishes to review alternative routes for a touring holiday, he would need a detailed road map marked with distances, place names, types of scenery, and so on. For a mineral prospector surveying the same area, this would be substantially less useful for his purpose: he would want a geological map. While neither map resembles closely the physical reality of the original that it represents, both may serve satisfactorily the purpose for which they were constructed. They abstract selectively from that reality.

Again, if a plane-builder wishes to gauge the flight characteristics of passenger aircraft he would use a wind tunnel, avoiding the expense and danger of the real environment for 'live' testing. And in it he places another model—the plane—which can depart in many details other than just size from the full-scale version: it need not be made from the same material as the real aircraft; paint colour is irrelevant; fully functioning engines are unnecessary; crew and personnel are superfluous to the exercise in hand. Even with all these major differences between the model and reality, the former can be used to explain a good deal about the latter. The areas in which it differs are not germane to the problems under analysis—experience and common sense tell us that. By a process of abstraction, the embellishments disappear to reveal the essential.

These models, however, relate to the material world. Some commentators[3] have objected to the use of models in the context of social sciences. They accept that the technique may be appropriate for physical experiment, but its utility in ascertaining and predicting behavioural relationships is doubted or denied. The proof of the pudding is, of course, in the eating, and it is easy to point to a number of econometric and demographic models that, while imperfect, do provide adequate indicators of the structure of the systems they seek to simulate. These could be compared to nineteenth-century maps of the interior of Africa, which provided sufficient information for further exploration and assisted materially in moving towards the more accurate and useful charts available today—though certainly even these are by no means perfect.

We can, however, go further than merely producing these empirical examples and assert that men think in terms of models.[4] Only by mental manipulation of experience can rational decisions be made about future courses of action. Those who do not think in this way are called insane. Furthermore, those who are commonly regarded as anarchic in their thinking may still be highly rational—a painter will still need to know from his experience the effect of mixing different colours or the appearance of applying different techniques. If his work is totally random it owes nothing to the painter's mind; it could be interesting in its effect, but this will be fortuitous.

Many critics object on the grounds that to model successfully in the social environment is so difficult as to render the attempt fruitless, not worth the effort. In 1974 the London *Economist*, under the title 'All the false prophets', showed how badly the experts had botched their forecasts.[5] World food production, raw material shortages and surpluses, the pace of technological development, and the supply of science graduates were all cited as examples not merely of inaccuracy, but indeed of a failure to make any meaningful prediction at all. In fact, during the 1960s considerable disservice was done to the science by the enthusiastic and excessive claims made for it by those who

3

thereby showed their lack of understanding of it. We certainly agree with those who reject the attempts to model the whole social universe.[6] The tools cannot, however, be discarded because the workmen (including the tool-makers) are ill-trained, or because the job is difficult. If we are to understand and hence to plan in our corner of the world, we have to make the effort to improve our skills to construct and use models.

The purpose of a scenario planning system

This book, then, is about making this effort in the field of the economic, social, and political environment of a multi-business corporation; that is to say, we are creating coherent pictures of different possible events in the environment and testing, through linked models, the impact of such changes upon a set of businesses. That is scenario planning. In our description, we shall be generalizing from our practical experience in actually building a scenario planning system—and we should add that this was done in the real world, not another of our duplicates: it was produced under conditons of commercial urgency with bullets pinging into the woodwork of our corporate bunk-house. But how could something so apparently mathematical be useful to managers, ducking for cover in this bunk-house, beseiged by an increasingly hostile and volatile economy? Why not let them adopt the tactics that a survey of the immediate terrain suggests, without worrying what is happening in more distant valleys or hills?

Corporations operate in numerous markets, whether as supplier or consumer, and movements in these markets affect both revenue and costs. Profits vary as a consequence, as does the future potential for developing the business. The markets are, therefore, the key building blocks of the corporate environment. It is tempting to divorce one market from another and, in making decisions, to view it in total isolation—like an archipelago of independent and isolated island communities. This is a false image. We shall come back frequently to this point: while all a corporation's businesses may operate in closely related markets, these markets are a part of the wider economic system, no longer even contained within national boundaries, but spilling over into the world at large. No corporation is dependent exclusively upon its own markets, its own microeconomic environment, but is inevitably involved with the broader system, known as the macroeconomic environment.

This is not an invitation to gaze into the hazy distance, where all detail is obscured. In fact, the system represents a means for achieving a clearer focus on what is important. The macroeconomy not only cycles, but is subject to shocks, normally from the political sphere. It is also slowly evolving and changing its characteristics under the impact of technological, social, and demographic developments. As each year goes by, national economies become

4

more dependent upon one another: more markets take on a greater world dimension. The manner in which developments in the macroeconomy impinge on the micro-environment and on how the corporation will be affected may be of material significance. So, a scenario planning system will define the complete environment first in terms of linked models of the macroeconomy of the relevant markets and then of the corporation itself. But since the executive, in his business rôle, is not conerned with political and economic events that have negligible impact upon his corporation, the well designed system will help to discriminate between those issues that are critical and those that are not.

This mechanism is invaluable, nowadays. Conjecture about the future of the macroeconomy and the social fabric of the country is never in short supply. A feature of modern journalism is that the inconsequential is often elevated to a crisis in the interests of selling newspapers or air-time. Moreover, the 'crisis' will have much greater news value if it seems imminent. We are made to live in a maelstrom of anticipation, continuously learning that we are on the brink of a new dark age. The past, by contrast, takes on a golden hue. The bemused executive resides in a state of perpetual concern for his corner of the world. He needs, therefore, tools, such as scenario planning, which will sift for him the important from the inconsequential.

The nature of the system

A scenario planning system simulates the effect of external pressures upon a corporation through its financial and business structure. Its main purpose is to provide managers with a test-bed for their plans within a practical time-scale. So a key concept in our approach is that any planning round must start with the plans and policies of those managers—what we shall call the 'base-case' plans. The models are then used to ascertain how the base-case plans and their underlying strategies respond to change.

In order to prepare those plans, assumptions in the form of a forecast will have to be made. These assumptions will include all sorts of policies as well as specific factors in the environment. The latter may be detailed or very general; they may be economic in nature (the course of commodity prices), or political (the course of economic policy); they may be made explicitly or implicitly. But in any event, they are vulnerable, some more than others. Assessments of this tend to be subjective. So scenarios seek to vary the assumptions of the base-case forecast in a material way, in order to explore the consequences. By varying the assumptions imposed upon the macro-model, upon the market models, or even upon the corporate financial model, a scenario can be generated and the results compared with the base case.

The sort of changes envisaged could be those controlled by the managers— for example, the level of debt–equity ratio, the premium payable upon acquisition, the investment in inventories relative to sales, the growing or shedding of market share. The ones we shall concentrate upon, however, are external to management control, such as inflation, exchange rates, and the impact of macroeconomic factors upon demand.

We must, however, differentiate the sorts of factors that we are considering from those contemplated by many other scenario-builders, such as the impact of long-term social change through attitudes to education, work, family life, and so on. It is our expressed purpose to give managers a manipulative tool. This means that we only go as far out in time, or as remote in the chain of causation, as is needed to provide these managers with timely warnings about the impact of critical environmental factors. While we may extrapolate our data for longish periods, this is only to magnify effects and facilitate choice between different policy options and assumptions. The reality, however, is that five to ten years is about the maximum lead time needed for most (but not all) business to take appropriate action. We avoid speculating, therefore, on the longer-term social and political movements.

So we model the structure of the organization and determine, as effectively as we can, how the changes will affect it over a five- to ten-year period. In doing this, we create a duplicate corporation with which the managers can experiment. By their own recognition of the results, the more outrageous 'go-getting' ambitions should be subdued, while the more timorous are steeled to take the plunge.

We are not trying to promote the system as a forecasting machine, in the sense of saying: 'Plug in all the data and our black box will tell you how the future is going to be.' While econometricians will continue to battle with their equations in an attempt to achieve greater accuracy in the mathematical simulations of markets and economies, both they and we recognize that at present we cannot begin to pretend to infallibility. An event that may be critical will be overlooked until it has had its impact—and then it may be too late. It will, nevertheless, be imported into newly specified equations, which will thereby be an improvement on the old; and these new equations will be used until the next 'unconnected' event hurtles from outer space into the conscious universe of the analysts. Thus it was, for example, with the wallcoverings industry in the UK. Had the managers realized the extent to which wallpaper was bought literally to cover the cracks (and the grime), they might have foretold that improved housing standards (and the Clean Air Act) would reduce the market dramatically. Fifteen years on they are wiser—and poorer.

Lack of adequate information, as well as perception, means, too, that the accuracy with which the modellers are able to reflect the influence of 'connected' events will be limited by the crudest part of the equation. Spurious precision is the refuge of the pedant and the tool of the con-man. If managers are to be persuaded to supplement intuition by systems such as the one to be

6

described, it won't help if we try to fool them about the precision that is achievable. It is vital in understanding scenario planning to appreciate that there must be a lack of precision, but that this is not critical to its utility. The system enables the manager to perceive the general direction and the extent to which corporate results will be affected by change. He must not expect numerate forecasts to give high levels of accuracy.

We emphasize, therefore, that the sort of information to be obtained from the models is a far cry from the pretended truths of the racing tipsters. We accept the Arab proverb that assures us that a prophet who claims he can foretell the future is a liar, even if he gets it right. So the models give answers of the nature 'if x, then y'; 'if there is a recession of the order of 3 per cent GDP decline, this is likely to result in . . . '. What cannot be done with any certainty is predict that there will be a recession of that order. In other words, by testing a range of possibilities, a set of outcomes can be built up to provide guidelines as to change within that range. They provide an informed basis for making judgements.

As a consequence of the inability to be either precise or certain, the system is most effectively used for measurement of relative, not absolute, values. If the time-horizon of a plan is put at ten years, or even five, it is easy to see that the absolute values for sales are likely to be wildly awry, since they are so substantially dependent on inflation rates. Furthermore, those components of sales—mix or volume—that ostensibly eliminate the inflation factor are highly susceptible to other external market forces. It is, nevertheless, quite feasible to produce projections that remain sufficiently valid *relative to one another*. So, a manager may make an assumption that inflation will rise by 12 per cent in year 1, 9 per cent in year 2, and so on, and he tests the impact upon his businesses. Then he thinks: but what if that's a wrong assumption (and it most likely is)? He tries others, maybe higher, maybe lower, and soon he gets the feeling of how robust his businesses and the strategies he has applied to them may be to this external factor. It is not necessary to believe any particular assumption; only that the values that do occur are likely to fall within the limits of his choice. Finally, he is able to say which sets of businesses perform more effectively than the remainder against specific assumptions. He knows how the activities perform relative to one another—a vital factor in managing a portfolio of businesses.

The shape of the system

So now we must describe the main features of the sort of system we use for simulating our corner of the universe. The simplest way to start the description is by imagining a cartwheel. The outer rim represents the universe. The hub is the corporation with which the system is concerned and it is constructed in the form of a financial model. All points in the universe are connected with one

7

another, but, as pointed out earlier, it is not feasible to build a model of the whole universe. Separate environmental models of its appropriate parts have to be developed—as many as the system architect wishes. These are represented by the points along the rim to which the spokes of the wheel are attached, and the spokes themselves constitute the linkages between them and the financial model at the hub. The corporation, therefore, receives messages from the universe as translated by the environmental models and channelled by the linkages.

Delving deeper into the environmental models to find what sort of creature they are, it is clear that their content is dictated by managerial need. The manager, in preparing his plans, will describe explicitly or implicitly his environment. In doing so, he is composing a trilogy. The three parts are, first, the general politico-economic climate; second, the specific market places from which he buys his goods or services; and third, the specific markets in which he sells. To describe this, however, we shall now have to increase the sophistication of our wheel and change it into something more closely approaching a movie-maker's idea of a space station (Fig. 1.1). The representation of the space station, as we ultimately constructed it in the figure, is not much more complicated than the simple wheel. It is modular, of course, so that as many more 'pods' may be added to it as the planning engineers decide they need. The environmental models now lie between the corporate hub and the universal rim, as bulges in the spokes and the rim is divided into a series of separate scenarios. The sub-systems labelled 'Macro-economy', 'Supply' and 'Demand' are devoted respectively to the three influences referred to as the manager's trilogy.

Looking first at macroeconomic factors, it is clear that these may have a direct impact upon a corporation. For example, the corporation's financial position will be immediately affected by exchange rate movement, if it has debts denominated in foreign currencies—particularly if these are unmatched by a corresponding value of assets in the relevant territory. Again, when it consolidates the profits and losses of foreign subsidaries into its domestic currency this will make a difference in its profit and loss account and balance sheet. Interest rates are another example of an economic aggregate that can be fed through directly to a company's financial position, via the cost of (most frequently short-term) borrowings. In structural terms, therefore, such inputs are channelled from the macroeconomic models directly to the corporate financial model at the centre of the system.

Macroeconomic factors will, however, have an influence on both of the other sub-systems. In addition to the direct effect of the exchange rate and other movements mentioned above, they may also exert an impact upon the market place through suppliers' prices, import competition and export opportunity. Recent events in the UK, for example, where in a relatively short span of time there has been a move in the sterling–dollar relationship from

1 : 1.5 to 1 : 2.3, have forcibly reminded UK manufacturers that what could be sold in overseas markets at the lower level doesn't stand a chance at the higher. It amounts to an uncontrolled 50 per cent rise in price.

Similarly, changes in supply-side markets of a corporation's business can have both a direct and an indirect influence. The direct effect of wage and raw material price increases will be to raise production costs. If, however, this rise is experienced by all competitors in this particular final goods market, it is

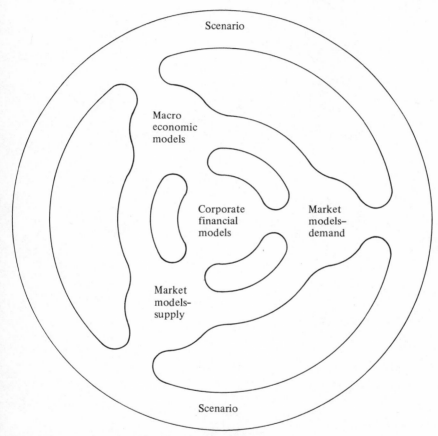

Figure 1.1 Structure of the planning system

possible that prices will also be increased and demand will react. So the demand side is affected indirectly, and this feeds through to volume sales of the business. Equally, it is possible to imagine, say, an increase in demand having both direct and indirect effects upon the business. The former would be reflected in increased sales (subject to capacity), but the latter might come via new entrants who, encouraged by expanding demand, depress margins.

9

Supply and demand models, therefore, interact and are not as independent as the diagram suggests. Nevertheless, it is convenient to trace the way in which influences are transmitted through the system as shown in Fig. 1.2.

Scenarios

The scenarios that are drawn in Fig. 1.2 have many of the characteristics of

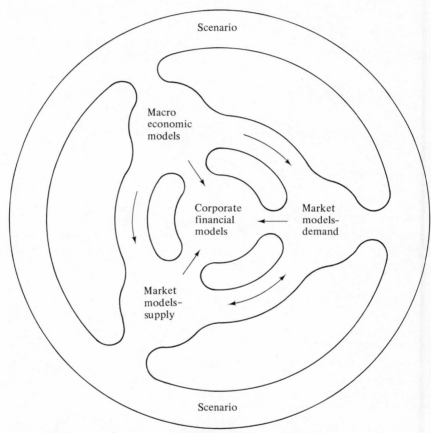

Figure 1.2 Transmission of influences through the planning system

forecasts in that, first, they are a presentation of a possible future outcome in the relevant corner of the universe; second, the components of the scenario must be consistent with one another so that they present a credible picture of that corner; and third, they are intended to be used as the basis for planning future action. In fact, the economic assumptions adopted as the base forecast can be termed a scenario, and in the system to be described this is called the 'base-case' scenario. The essential difference, however, between forecasts and scenarios for our purposes is that the former are used on the basis that they represent the highest probability of future outcomes in the minds of the planners at the time of their adoption; scenarios, on the other hand, only indicate possible outcomes, though certainly, for practical reasons, those that would be expected to have a major impact.

Scenario-building starts with an intuitive view of those factors that may have an effect upon the businesses that the corporation runs and upon its financial structure as a whole. They are, as indicated above, a picture of a small part of the universe which is developed into a consistent set of assumptions. The mechanisms by which assumptions, expressed in such vague terms as 'a Middle East crisis', are translated into projected values for wholesale prices, gross domestic products (GDP), consumer expenditure, etc., are discussed later in detail.

In general terms, it involves taking some of the equations contained in the macroeconomic models and manipulating them so as to represent the initial impact of the scenario. The model allows these influences to work themselves through the entire system. This process re-emphasizes the virtues of a formal model. By projecting the consequences of a wide range of economic variables, the dangers of environmental risk are exposed. The focus is not just on the immediate area of impact, for instance higher oil prices on energy costs, but on the effect on aggregate demand, exchange rates, domestic prices, interest rates, and so on. Furthermore, in manipulating the model and observing the intermediate results that emerge, new problems and consequences are posed, leading to further refinement of the scenario. Once again, the formal structure obliges the user to contemplate events in their entirety and not fall prey to purely parochial perspectives.

The approach has one great advantage over the practice of placing ranges on a few selected economic variables. The micro-models and other linkages will show that even the smallest corporation is vulnerable to a significant number of economic aggregates that are related to each other. When one aggregate is rising, another may necessarily be falling; thus, the size and character of any change in the environment cannot be caught by simple ranges. A scenario simulated on models should, however, capture these cross-cutting influences.

In summary, therefore, we have an overall structure for filtering the environmental influences and a means of projecting the future whereby we can beat to some extent our inability to predict. The purpose is to set as wide a scene for decision-taking by the corporate manager as is reasonably possible. It is important to recognize that scenario planning, as described in this book, owes its design to a combination of disciplines. Economists, econometricians, accountants, statisticians, mathematicians, political analysts, systems designers, and computer programmers all play a technical rôle. Each, on

11

reading this book, should perceive where his own contribution would be effective. Managers, on the other hand, must be generalists. There is no way they could construct and operate such a system on their own. There is no need for them to learn the techniques of building or maintaining it. What they have to know is what the capabilities of the system are and how it can be used in the business. The following descriptions, therefore, seek to strike a balance between a conceptual overview with some worked examples and a critical analysis of the technicalities which both limit and enlarge the scope of this approach. The more esoteric of these technicalities, however, we have tried to confine to Appendix 4.

Notes

1. Brian Silcock, 'The truth about Henry Abbott and his village', *Sunday Times*, 9 December 1979.
2. Dr S. Schoeffler, R. D. Buzzell, and D. F. Heary, 'Impact of strategic planning on profit performance', *Harvard Business Review*, March/April 1974.
3. Sir K. Popper, *The Poverty of Historicism*, Routledge & Kegan Paul, London, 1961; R. G. Collingwood, *The Idea of History*, Oxford University Press, Oxford, 1946.
4. K. W. Deutsch, 'Mechanisms and organisms in society', *Philosophy of Science*, **18**, 230–252, 1950.
5. For evidence that artists think and work in terms of models and archetypes see E. H. Gombrich, *Art and Illusion*, 5th edn., Phaidon Paperback, London, 1977.
6. Popper, op. cit.

2.
The accounting models

The corporate financial structure

At the hub of our space station lies the financial model of the Corporation. The model depicts the financial characteristics of the corporation in terms of accounting variables that are familiar to businessmen. Accountancy is, therefore, the first specialist discipline encountered in this multi-disciplinary exercise. Some knowledge of the profit and loss account (P & L) and balance sheet is assumed.[1] The normal accountancy conventions are shown schematically in Fig. 2.1 for those with only a rusty familiarity. In fact, a manager with just a little practice could program even a pocket calculator to derive these parameters to describe the financial performance of his business. A simple example of such a program (written by a manager) is included in Appendix 2.

The top part of the diagram deals with the profit and loss account items. Starting with sales, there are deducted the cost of sales and overheads, to give trading profit. Investment income, extraordinary items, and interest payable are then input to reach profit before tax, and finally tax is deducted, giving profit after tax. The lower half of the chart considers the balance sheet: working capital is made up from its components of inventories, receivables, and payables and then fixed assets at cost less accumulated depreciation. These total to the trading capital. The other balance sheet items, e.g., debt, cash, taxation and dividends payable, goodwill, and so on, complete the picture.

The manager who builds such a model for himself can gain real benefits. First, it gives him a much clearer picture of the way the business works as a financial system. Second, he only has to input a dozen factors to extract an array of useful information, including key ratios for measurement of performance. Figure 2.1 shows those ratios that are critical to a holding company reviewing a number of businesses in a mixed portfolio. If, on the other hand, a manager wanted to assess other factors, such as gross margin, inventories to sales, or receivables to sales, it is easy to see how a more detailed analysis of costs and working capital could enable this to be done. At the same time, where attention is focused on running the business at the coal face rather than in the money market, items such as debt–equity ratio, return on equity, or gearing could be omitted from the model.

Such a simplified model can, therefore, be very useful. Indeed, provided the manager knows the impact in financial terms, it could be used for some 'what if' type questions by manipulation of, say costs or investment. For example, provided the employment cost is known, the impact of a wages rise in his business—say a 20 per cent increase compared with plan—could be

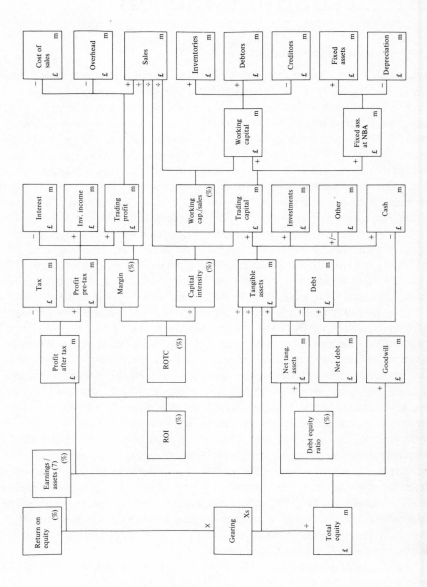

Figure 2.1 Capital, profit, and ratio analysis

ascertained on profit and net margin and on the overall return. If, however, as is likely, such wages rise emanates from general increases in the labour market, triggered by inflation in consumer prices, then merely to show cost increases would be to tell only a small part of the story. The financial figures alone cannot tell much about the dynamics of the business or its place in larger market and economic systems. A set of complex models is required for this, and the financial model at the centre has to be constructed in a way that enables it to respond in a wide variety of components to a multiplicity of external stimuli.

A senior manager is well advised, tracing through his own program like the one indicated in Fig. 2.1, to keep on top of the concepts with which his accounting and computing staff will have to grapple. Awareness of the limitations of accounting identities, and of the areas where there is a need to formulate dynamic relationships, is fundamental to managing the design of this component of the scenario planning system. Direct involvement is desirable for two reasons: first, it impresses upon the technicians the need to design a system that non-technicians can use; second, it grounds the manager sufficiently in the system to explain (and defend) it. A manager responsible for such a system can be confident of one thing: it will be questioned and probed thoroughly by allies and enemies alike!

Features of the financial model

The basic intention behind the financial model is to use it as a tool for planning by exploring change from a base-case. It is not intended primarily to fulfil a corporate accounting purpose. Although it incorporates many financial functions, sometimes of considerable complexity, it is not constructed as a consolidation model. General assumptions may be used, for example, as to tax and interest rates. A consolidation routine should be incorporated into the system in order that an overall view of the impact of a scenario upon the corporation can be taken, but it will not be necessary to adopt the precision of a formal accounting consolidation.

The financial structure within the model is built up by reference not only to the profit and loss account and balance sheet, but also to the cash flow. Referring again to the simplified structure in Fig. 2.1, this may be illustrated as in Fig. 2.2, taking it only so far as the trading level. Cash flow is among the most important information available for assessing the well-being of a company over a period of time, because it is information that is least dependent upon accounting judgement. At the risk of torturing our space analogy, it is like the pole star around which rational space navigation will revolve. While it is true that, like all other company data, it does not tell a complete story, nevertheless, all other figures have to reconcile ultimately with the actuality of the cash flow. It is, therefore, vital to provide this as a major output of any planning system.

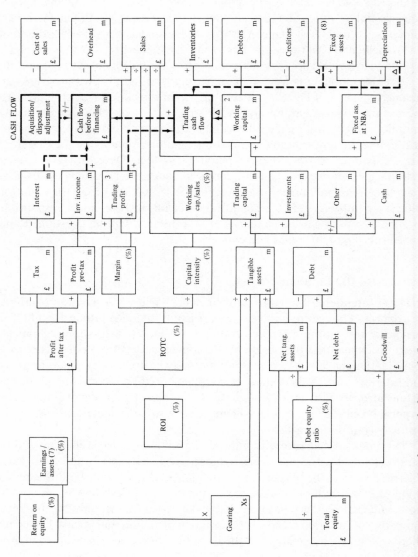

Figure 2.2 Analysis including cash flow

Geographical analysis

The location of production facilities will have a major impact upon the character of the data needed for scenario manipulation. For example, the tax rate and the timing of tax payments varies from country to country. In many, tax is payable during the year in which it is incurred on an instalment basis.[2] Similarly, where a limitation is placed upon the repatriation of profits, as for instance in Brazil,[3] it may give a false impression if the model aggregates cash flow of the group from all sources so that it is assumed to be readily available anywhere in the world. Consequently, the model has to set up separate compartments to deal with each of the various tax and exchange control jurisdictions in which the organization has a significant operation. A further technicality, which, for similar reasons, may be dealt with in the same way, are those activities run as subsidiary companies, with minority shareholders. Clearly, their cash flow cannot be treated as belonging to the organization, however tempting its assimilation may be! Indeed, in including such non-wholly owned subsidaries, it is essential to ensure that only P & L and balance sheet effects, plus dividends and loan transactions, are recorded.

Apart from the structural requirements dictated by these technical points, there is a need, in scenario planning, to differentiate between the major economies within which the organization operates, whether as a buyer of raw materials or a supplier of goods. As is evident, inflation, exchange rates, growth, and many other factors vary considerably from place to place. It would be absurd to apply the changes in the UK rate of inflation to businesses in the USA. So there must be a territory-by-territory analysis.

For all the foregoing reasons, therefore, the base-plan information should be categorized by territory of production and (separately) of sales. This, however, could involve a lot of detail. To what level of detail should the analysis aspire? Many multinationals are represented in a very large number of locations. For instance, our own UK corporation was represented recently by specific establishments in over 30 countries, but it took over 95 per cent of its sales and profit from only 7 of these. It would be a waste of time for the top management of that corporation to be concerned in detail, therefore, with scenarios for the remaining 23. Data collection is expensive; unnecessary data collection leads to mutiny among those asked to supply it and suffocation of those trying to use it.

There is, however, no absolute rule on how much detail to suppress: only the guideline that, if the objective is to be able to perceive how change will affect the total group (or any part under review), ignore those territories that will not make any significant impact upon the totality—or, perhaps, if in aggregate they do make a difference, they may be put in as a residual unit.

17

Analysis by business unit

In the preceding paragraphs we have indicated how to compartmentalize the financial structure of a group to deal with matters affecting its overall cash flow and geographical location. But cash flow is the end result of running the business. We now have to look at the question, 'What is the business that is being run?' Reference has been made earlier to 'activities' and to 'consolidation'. These presuppose a number of different businesses and indeed, in almost any but the smallest trading organization, the operation can be subdivided by reference to sales in a number of different market places. The organization should, therefore, be analysed into units representing the highest level at which an individual market strategy can be properly formulated. We call such units 'activities'.

A market, very broadly, is the arena within which the price for a good or service is set.[4] A market strategy is of the form: increase, reduce, or maintain a share of that market (or a segment of it). The apparent simplicity of this definition, however, is a trap. Anyone who has tried knows that there is no unambiguous way in practice to specify markets. For example, a book publishing company might subdivide the business into fiction and non-fiction. Fiction may then be further partitioned into classics, detective, romance, western, and so on. Whether these are separate markets in any meaningful way must be for the judgement of the operating managers—once they understand the purpose of the enquiry. Furthermore, it makes no sense to adopt a blanket strategy of simultaneously increasing share rapidly in recognized separate markets. In one market, demand may be declining fast; in another, competition may have wrecked margins; in a third, a virtual monopoly may be already enjoyed. It is these market strategy considerations that dictate the analysis of the organization into separate activities.

In practice, however, there is a limit to the application of this principle in scenario planning. There just may not be information available at the microeconomic level to enable differentiation between market sectors. In the UK, for example, the information relating to book publishing would not admit of the ability to manipulate any of the above components of consumer book publishing individually against changes in the environment. On the other hand, there is no particular reason for believing that a recession would affect, say, science fiction more than any other form. Perhaps the sci-fi titles might need to be more escapist and lurid—'Godzilla meets Bambi'—but this is an issue of coping tactically with the situation and does not raise strategic issues about market share. So there is no point in disaggregating for scenario planning purposes beyond the level of meaningful differentiation. Nevertheless, scenario planning is only part of the total planning process, and disaggregation will, therefore, be pursued to the appropriate level for *strategic* purposes.

Since the rule requires that the analysis be undertaken at the *highest* level at which a market strategy may be set, this often means that activities that have been thought of as separate should be aggregated for planning purposes. Where is the point in trying to establish independently a strategy for a printing works that serves exclusively or substantially the book publishing activities above? The printery grows or declines with the book business. The numbers should be put together to make sure that that piece of the business is giving adequate returns as a whole. In other words, where there is genuine vertical integration, the integrated businesses must be treated as one.

A similar problem emerges when export markets are considered. If there is a single plant manufacturing glassware in Holland, whose capacity is devoted largely to the Dutch market, but which also sells into Germany, France, Belgium—and even into 'deep-sea' markets—it cannot, in practice, be treated as a series of separate activities: the complexity and information required to do so would be out of proportion to the materiality of the results. The test must, as always, be the extent to which change in any particular factor will affect the overall results that are to be projected. If the difference is trivial, it should be ignored. In the case given, some suitably weighted correlation must be attempted. The message, however, is clear: it is difficult to define an activity by a rigid universal rule; rarely will the market definitions used by the corporation square exactly with the statistics available. Judgement must be used to apply those definitions and those statistics that will give a sufficiently valid answer upon which action may be founded with reasonable confidence.

In practice, it is unfortunate for planners that almost all corporate reward systems are based on the size of the activity—measured either in sales or investments terms—and on the short-term profit or cash flow achievement, usually just the year last past. As a result, considerable resistance may be encountered to dissecting the corporate carcase in the revealing way outlined above. The successful fiction publisher would certainly not want his high returns to be contaminated by the losses of the printers of his product. Yet, being in charge of the whole fiction division, he might reject attempts to report separately on each of his publishing market sectors, to avoid the perhaps inevitable truncation of this empire, when it becomes apparent that certain parts have been steadily losing money for years. Until a proper analysis of business activities has been undertaken, however, it is not possible to establish appropriate strategies (or, incidentally, a proper reward system directed towards achievement). So at some point, superior management may have to jump into the ring and say: 'This is how it's going to be!'

Another group of people who may obstruct the suitable analysis of a set of businesses are the accountants who work in them. Before they arise as a body to burn this book, let us admit they have reason to be vigilant. The greater part of the load of information-gathering in most organizations falls upon them. They will, quite properly, object to consolidating and analysing more

19

information than they believe to be appropriate. A considerable problem in this context is the allocation of shared costs. If a number of different activities are carried on in a factory—suppose, for example, it is a paper-mill making pulp, newsprint, and fine papers—the problem is difficult. Nevertheless, unless it is solved, a realistic statement of costs and hence margins for each line of business cannot be established. It is, of course, unnecessary to allocate costs to the last penny or cent, and it is relatively easy to derive rule-of-thumb methods to avoid detailed calculation—energy by output volumes, accommodation by floor space, welfare by employees, and so on. Whatever mechanisms are adopted, however, the exercise must be undertaken.

One further remark using the publishing and printing business earlier discussed. Once the level of return from the aggregated activities falls below an acceptable level, then it becomes appropriate again to think of the possiblities of separating them. If market opportunities were to present themselves for major profitable external print work, then again it may be right to reconsider the individual strategies for the parts: potentially there may be a case for them to cease to be treated as vertically integrated. So they re-emerge as discrete strategic business units.

There is, too, another practical benefit that occurs from the separation of the group into individual market-based activities. This is that it enables complete flexibility in reviewing the portfolio for strategic purposes. Any disposals can be simulated, any acquisitions can be hypothetically included, any sets of businesses can be examined on their own. This represents a most powerful tool in the hands of those whose job it is to consider 'what-if' type questions relating to the shape of the organization as a whole. And they may do it with reasonable confidence that the internal implications in terms of inter-company trading, sharing of services, and so on have been adequately taken into account.

Business dynamics

The earlier discussion of the simple financial model described in Fig. 2.1 points to the reality that the conventional accounting framework, though familiar and useful, is no more than a set of static definitions which by themselves give no indication of how the financial performance of a business will be affected by a change in the environment. Behavioural or reaction rules are needed to change the financial variables in accordance with a new environment. The rules will reflect changes that flow through a number of financial components of the system on the assumption either that a policy relating to business ratios will be maintained (e.g., that inventory to sales ratios will be held) or, conversely, that such policy cannot reasonably be maintained (e.g., that margins will be reduced to maintain adequate volume to survive). The financial model must be able to change key variables in both the P & L account

20

and the balance sheet, singly and simultaneously if necessary. Furthermore, these changes must be internally consistent with the new environment postulated by the model.

Trading profit is the simple difference between sales and costs; so to measure how a scenario will affect it, the impact upon each component must be estimated. In Chapter 1 mention was made of market models—that is, models of the market in which the company participates as supplier or consumer. These models take a postulated change in the macroeconomy and transmit it to a change in each of the markets. The supply side, dealing with the costs of the business, may well be an integral feature of models capable of simulating market sales. In some cases the supply costs and the demand side may be treated separately.

The first step, therefore, in converting the inert accounting definitions into a dynamic behavioural model of the corporation is to devise equations that relate changes in sales volumes and prices in the market place to adjusted sales volumes and prices in the business. Provided that there is reasonable congruity between the total market as simulated by the market models and the market sales defined for the purposes of the plan, the movement of one element relative to the other is calculated by reference to the market share. A neutral stance (which is also the simplest) assumes that both the selling price and sales volume in the business will rise by the same percentage as the total market counterparts. In the absence of historic evidence to the contrary, the simple link may be the best, so there will be an equation in the financial model of the following form:

$$V_s = V_b \, (MV_s/MV_b)$$

and
$$P_s = P_b \, (MP_s/MP_b) \qquad (2.1)$$

where V denotes volume sales of the activity; MV is market volume sales, P is selling price of the activity; MP is aggregate market selling price, while the subscript b denotes base case and s the scenario value, i.e., a proposed alternative value.

It is worth digressing to show the reason for having a base-case founded upon market strategies. It becomes apparent from the algebraic form. The management in a particular business might be pursuing a strategy of expanding market share such that

$$V_b/MV_{bt} < V_b/MV_{bt+1} \ldots V_b/MV_{bt+n} \qquad (2.2)$$

where t is time. The strategy is to be achieved by steadily reducing the relative price of the product:

$$P_b/MP_{bt} > P_b/MP_{bt+1} > \ldots > P_b/MP_{bt+n}. \qquad (2.3)$$

The changes reflecting the new environment leave that strategy intact in relative terms. The manager can now answer the question, 'What will be the

21

results of my strategy if it is pursued in an alternative environment?' What it does not answer is the question, 'What is the best strategy under these new circumstances?' Some passing reference is made to the manner in which strategies are determined in later chapters (though it must be the subject of a book in its own right). All the scenario exercise does is indicate that a strategy will hold under a variety of circumstances. For this reason a certain amount of tactical response to the new environment must be built into the financial model to make it realistic. This is illustrated a little later, but let us return to the assumption that links the change in total market sales to activity sales.

The simple assumption of linking changes in activity sales to changes in total demand works well enough when the market is essentially protected from foreign competition. When international trade is involved, in the context either of exports or of foreign competition in the domestic market, the position is more difficult. The competitiveness and hence fortunes of an industry can be altered, sometimes quite dramatically, by the roulette wheel of economic change. Demand for a product in the home market could be quite strong, but domestic producers might not be enjoying the growth because they are uncompetitive. Linking the activity's sales solely to changes in demand, under a scenario that has made home producers uncompetitive, would make the performance of the business appear more favourable than it would otherwise be. The activity volume component would, in such case, be linked to output of domestic producers and the price to the home selling price. The market price, in a well specified model of the market, would also be influenced by foreign costs and prices. A squeeze from abroad might come because market prices, held down through foreign competition, do not rise with domestic costs, or by the loss of domestic sales volume, or by some combination of the two. Much the same argument applies to exports, and it is important to ensure, where relevant, that the data provided for the base-case plan discriminate between principal export markets.

Cost dynamics

Changing sales revenue affects only one side of the gross trading profit equation, the other side being costs. Even if unit costs had not altered between scenarios, the movement in output volume would require some modification in the quantity of inputs consumed in production. If the scenario raised output, then more raw materials, energy and perhaps labour might have to be consumed. The financial model of the business must therefore have some rules (or equations), to guide the cost side, consistent with the impact of the scenario upon the various markets in which the company operates.

Costs can be classified into fixed and variable. Fixed costs do not vary with output volume and would include such items as local authority rates, heating,

22

water and light, insurance, etc. There may also be other substantial expenses which can be varied but in effect are relatively inelastic with respect to output. If these two are combined into a singled fixed-cost element, assumed not to vary with output, then it will change in aggregate only when inflation varies from the base-case. Algebraically,

$$FC_s = FC_b \, (I_s/I_b) \tag{2.4}$$

where FC is the fixed cost component and I is a suitable general index of inflation. The choice of inflation index poses some problems, since the mix of items to which it will be applied will inevitably be unique. In the absence of a purpose-built index, something like the retail price index may serve well enough.

The remaining cost items all vary with output as well as with inflation. They can be divided into three main categories: labour costs, energy costs, and raw material costs. There is, in fact, no reason why they could not be subdivided further—the last might be a particular candidate for subdivision. Consider first the impact of a rise in volume relative to base consequent upon a scenario. The quantity of labour consumed (man-hours) in production will be some function of output:

$$VL=f\,(VO) \tag{2.5}$$

where VL is the volume of labour and VO the volume of output. The precise relationship between labour inputs and output is determined by the technology of production. In many continuous-process industries with high capital intensity, the machines can merely be set at a faster pace and output increased with virtually no increase in the quantity of labour. In other industries, perhaps the only way to raise output is by taking on commensurate labour. However, assuming a given quantity of plant and capital equipment, the amount of additional output produced by each increment of labour will diminish as the plant reaches capacity. A wide range of curves relating the quantity of labour and output are conceivable, but only one will be given by the particular plant concerned.

Curve (a) in Fig. 2.3 might be the type associated with a continuous process industry. A certain amount of labour is required before any output can be produced, but then output will rise rapidly for a small increase in hours worked. However, as maximum capacity is reached output is hardly increased at all, no matter what the increase in labour. Curve (b) still has diminishing marginal return as full capacity is reached. However, over most of its range a steady increase in output can only be achieved with a steady increase in labour. On the other hand, curve (c) shows that at low levels of output, quite large increases in labour hardly raise production; thereafter, output rises very quickly for little additional labour force. It is important to have some idea of the relationship between changes in output and labour. A cost accountant or

23

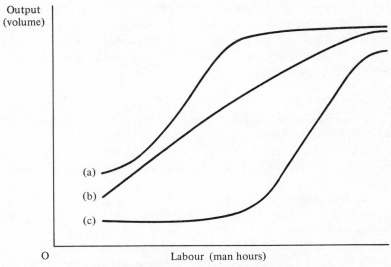

Figure 2.3 Relationship of quantity of labour and output

production manager will readily produce an approximate curve or enough information for one to be constructed.

Once an equation of the functional relationship expressed in Fig. 2.3 is available, it becomes possible to estimate how the quantity of labour will change as a result of, say, the increased output resulting from a scenario. The estimate may well be crude, and over some ranges of the curve particular issues may be raised. For instance, at very low levels of output labour redundancies may be unavoidable, and severance payments may have to be paid on a large scale. It is not impossible to devise some rule to cope with this difficulty. However, this degree of refinement may not be necessary. There is little point in devising a system in which any component is more refined than the crudest parts. Devising the scenarios themselves requires a great deal of judgement and guesswork, and it is as well to remember this as the building blocks of the system are being designed.

Similar problems are raised by the treatment of energy costs. Some production processes have energy usage that hardly varies with output. Kilns have to be kept at the correct temperature to bring about the physical change in the products they are heating. The amount of energy needed in these circumstances will therefore not vary directly with the number of products put through the kiln. In other industries, there may be a very constant relationship between changes in energy consumption and movements in output. Once again, some research might be needed to provide the precise equation for the following functional equation:

24

$$VE = f(VO) \qquad (2.6)$$

where VE is the volume of energy consumed.

The volume of raw materials used in production will in most cases bear a fairly constant relationship with the level of output, such that the scenario volume of raw materials used can be determined thus:

$$VR_s = VR_b\,(VO_s/VO_b) \qquad (2.7)$$

where VR is the volume of raw materials consumed. Once again, the production technology determines the real relation between raw material used and output, and if there are reasons for believing they are not linearly related, then a better approximation will be required.

The unit cost of each input, or at least the dominant ones, can be directly determined from their market price as simulated by the appropriate price model. A papermaker relying on pulp as his principal raw material (rather than on waste), would need a price model for raw materials to simulate a scenario change. The same would be true of energy costs and perhaps even for wages if there were good reasons to believe this would diverge from the national norm in terms of percentage changes. Linking the price of the inputs to a suitable price index generated by the scenario will ensure that costs move according to the new assumptions.

Investment in capacity

Although both revenue and cost components have been discussed, there are certain remaining issues as regards volume changes. What happens when a scenario change implies an increase in output beyond capacity? Obviously, sales cannot be permitted to exceed maximum capacity. The issue is one of planning philosophy. The base-case plan reflects the strategy the local management intends to pursue. If the market strategy is to raise market share, and, *inter alia*, this implies investing in additional plant, what adjustments need to be made if the scenario market growth rate is much faster than in the base-case? It may be that, even with the planned additional plant, it is not possible to maintain market share, let alone increase it.

The dilemma can be dealt with in one of two ways. The first is not to attempt any adjustment whatsoever, but merely to flag the situation that under the scenario the growth in business sales volume is lower than projected market growth rates. This is the least complicated option and serves the purpose of informing the corporation that the strategy is not robust to that particular scenario and affords them the chance of reviewing that aspect of the plan. The second option requires expanding capacity by raising investment such that the business is not restrained in the scenario by a lack of plant. This raises several problems. First, an algorithm is required to convert additional output requirements into additional investment, labour, and other inputs. In economic terms, a production function is needed.[5] For a given level of output this equation would provide the corresponding inputs. The construction of these functions on an industry basis is not without its difficulties but has been attempted in a variety of areas, and they would provide a shot at the additional investment needed.

The phasing of the additional investment also presents a difficulty. The investment expenditure must precede the additional output requirement by an appropriate lag: a certain period is required before new capacity comes on stream. If these problems can be solved, bearing in mind that the margin of error in scenario planning is inevitably wide, so that too great a precision is not needed, then it would be possible to maintain the integrity of the market strategy. On balance, however, we would favour the first approach for its simplicity.

Of course, market growth under a scenario could be a lot lower than plan. If additional capacity were being built to meet strong demand under the base-case, then the lower growth scenario will result in a far lower return on trading capital than promised. This again should be flagged by the model, although, as with too little capacity, adjustments could be made to investment plans. Investment under the scenario could be cut back by the use of a suitable production function. Technical modelling problems are undoubtedly raised by capacity changes, but, again, a more important philosophical planning issue emerges. Is the aim of the scenario planning system to redraw the plans in line with a proposed alternative environment, or is it to flag the problem areas that require management discussion and consideration? Our view is that it should be the latter, and so the financial models should seek to reflect how management might normally react to the changed economic environment while attempting to fulfil the broad outline of the strategy contained in the base case. So, some adjustment (as discussed) is seen as necessary on sales and revenue, but not in fixed capital investment. The same is not true, however, for working capital.

Two influences determine inventory levels.[6] The first is that planned component which corresponds to normal working requirements, given an assumed level of sales; the second is an involuntary component which arises when the assumption about sales goes awry. If the economy suddenly turns down and sales slump, a large part of output will be going into inventory, at least until output is reduced. The base-case plan for inventories will contain the planned ratio of inventory to output. Thus, if sales fall under the scenario, planned inventories would still be given by this ratio. In reality, however, the ratio would rise, and this needs to be simulated. The market models could contain an inventory equation for the industry as a whole which would allow a direct adjustment to the ratio. Algebraically,

$$S_s/VO_s = S_b/VO_v \ (IO_s/IO_b)$$

where S/VO is the activity inventory-to-output ratio and IO is the inventory output ratio of domestic producers in the relevant industry. If this is not possible—sometimes data are not available—a crude device such as using manufacturers' or distributors' inventory to output ratios could be used as appropriate. The second option is obviously less acceptable than the first.

A similar problem to that encountered in simulating a standard policy response on inventories arises in the context of receivables—whether it is to be assumed that, inevitably, on the downside of the cycle, day's credit will extend, or to adhere to the more optimistic policy of the rigid period of payment. On balance, we consider that the difficulty of formalizing a behavioural rule that will hold good in a variety of circumstances is such as to lead in this area (and, indeed, in payables) to maintaining plan policy without variation—but so that payables and receivables will vary with input and output volumes respectively. We shall indicate in Chapter 7 how, by pulling various levers such as day's credit, the individual impact of a change in any particular policy can be demonstrated. This approach is probably sufficient to deal with the response of the business in the area of monetary working capital to changes in the environment.

The rules for moving other cash variables, such as interest payments or the exchange rate, for consolidation purposes or repayment of foreign debt are self-evident. The new scenario will have exchange and interest rates which can be applied to the base-case to produce scenario values. The remaining financial variables, such as depreciation and taxation, will follow the accounting and taxation rules applying at the time.

The financial model, therefore, requires an accounting structure, consistent with a detailed P & L account, balance sheet and cash flow statement in which sales and cost data are organized by the country of sale and place of manufacture. The definitions and identities used to derive a full financial statement are embodied in the model. However, in addition to these 'passive' accounting rules, there are certain business behaviour equations that link through changes in the environment to the financial parameters of the business. This structure, then, can work upon the plan data input by managers at activity, divisional, and corporate level to simulate how the external world will modify those plans. The next step is to take a look at the plan data and consider what is needed and how it may be manipulated in practice.

Notes

1. A clear guide is given in Leon Simons, *The Basic Arts of Financial Management*, Business Books Ltd, London, 1974.
2. An example is Canada: see *Business Study Canada*, Touche Ross International, New York, 1975, p. 125.
3. *Business Study Brazil*, Touche Ross International, New York, 1973, p. 27.

4. A much fuller description is available in the *PIMS Data Manual*, Strategic Planning Institute, Boston, 1978.
5. G. C. Harcourt and N. F. Laing, *Capital and Growth*, Penguin Books, Harmondsworth, 1971; see ch. 5 for an econometric approach.
6. R. C. O. Matthews, *The Trade Cycle*, Cambridge University Press, Cambridge, 1959.

3.
The business data base

Information needs

From time to time, you may come across a corporate headquarters pretty well comatose, like a well-fed boa constrictor, as it seeks to digest all the mass of information it has engorged. As we said before, the amount of data fed into the system needs to be limited. So how much data needs to be gathered? The following description represents a pragmatic view of the minimum business data base necessary for managers to get a sufficient description of each activity and of the whole organization for scenario planning.

Ideally, a scenario planning system would be well developed before asking for the data. When the requirements are known, rather than anticipated, the inevitable result is a rather shorter shopping list than otherwise. However, self-censorship at the design stage, out of a belief that the activity staff would not have the best data, can lead to needless restrictions and an over-generalized model. At one stage during the development of our own system, for instance, we were concerned to separate energy costs from all other variable non-labour costs and then to devise a way of linking the volume of energy consumed in production with final output. We opted for the broadest definition conceivable, to try and save our business planners time and effort. Inevitably, one of them phoned back, concerned about the work involved because it would have meant aggregating the various categories into which he had already analysed his energy expenditure. Furthermore, it transpired that he had also developed algorithms for each such category. Sometimes it pays to ask the more detailed question first.

In terms of time span, it is commonly said that information should cover as long a past period as future projections. This, though, must be thought of as the minimum. Many business plans adopt, quite reasonably, a three-year time horizon, but three years of past data will not cover a full economic cycle, and is inadequate, therefore, for the purpose of assessing trends for scenario planning. A five-year annual history is preferable—and even that is a slim sample. When starting up a new planning system, planners ought to get information as far back as the tolerance of their colleagues supplying the data will allow. Once the system is implemented, of course, the problem reduces year by year. After ten years, there will be an information span that will be the envy of corporate neighbours.

Activity analysis

Now we come to look at the detail required from each activity. This book is concerned with scenario planning, and not with the generation of long-term strategies. We avoid, therefore, any detailed discussion of that part of our data base devoted to strategy formulation. Nevertheless, in considering the necessary set of information for scenario purposes, remarks about 'strategy data' creep in, and we also deal to a degree with factors relating to the monitoring of performance, because these may be the appropriate way to perceive the impact of a change in the environment. The diagram in Fig. 2.1 indicated a rudimentary financial structure and nominated certain inputs. These remain basically the items that need to be collected, but necessarily they have to be supplemented by more detail to answer the more complex problems to which we have referred. So the general shopping list, by main headings, is as follows. (Definitions are included in Appendix 1.) All data should be stated in the principal currency of the activity.

Data for activity analysis
1. Sales • total external to activity
         • total external to group
2. Costs • energy
         • raw materials
         • employment
         • central charges
         • extraordinary
3. Activity profit
4. Activity cash flow
5. Working capital • total average
                   • inventories average
6. Fixed assets • at cost
                • at net book amount
                • depreciation
                • capital expenditure
7. Non-financial data • number of employees
                      • volume index
                      • capacity utilization

Sales and costs
The starting point is 'Sales', of which there are two important categories:

• sales external to the activity (activity sales)
• sales external to the group (group sales)

The former is used in calculating performance of the activity in a manner that enables comparison with all other activities in the corporate portfolio. Take the example of a foundry that sells 15 per cent of its output to a metal converter within the group, which sells all of its output externally. It would be misleading to base the calculation of their respective margins on group sales. In the case in

Table 3.1 the converter has the better margin. The reduction in sales to exclude the amount sold internally benefits the foundry's margin, but this is an illusion and is irrelevant in the measurement of relative performance.

The whole question of inter-company sales is fraught with all sorts of political traps. Volumes have been written about the proper assessment of internal transfer prices. In our own organization, this was a particularly pointed argument at one time between printers and publishers and between paper-makers and packagers. The tendency was for the managerially dominant activity to depress or raise the price below or above economic levels, even though management swore that arm's-length market prices were being charged. At all events, some caution has to be exercised in using inter-company prices as a yardstick for comparisons.

Group sales are essential for consolidation; such information may be aggregated at any level within the group; the choice will be dictated by the management hierarchy and the points at which control is to be exerted. But whether sales are taken external to a set of activities, to a division, or to the

Table 3.1

| | Sales | | Activity | Margin | |
	Activity	Group	profit	Activity	Group
	£'000	£'000	£'000	%	%
Foundry	10 000	8500	1000	10	12
Converter	5000	5000	550	11	11

group as a whole, the only sales value that is valid for comparison of trading performance is 'sales external to activity'.

Sales figures must also be subdivided into all major export markets that are material (in the way described in Chapter 2). In general, however, information of this nature is most effectively dealt with as a note on the schedules, rather than attempting to generalize its format.

Costs and profit

Knowledge of costs plays a vital part in assessing environmental impacts: raw materials, wages, energy, and so on are all affected by external circumstances. A quick evaluation of, say, a 20 per cent oil price rise can be calculated by reference to the proportion of total costs that energy represents prior to the rise. If the proportion is high, the alarm bells will ring at once. But in any case, this is only the first and easy part of the exercise. The second is the assessment of the influence of the trigger event upon demand for the corporation's products. So it is the combination of sales and cost information that ultimately enables the full horror (or delight) of the changing environment to be perceived.

Activity profit is calculated by deducting from activity sales all attributable costs thereto, including depreciation, but not interest, extraordinary costs or central charges. The reason for taking the pre-interest figure is to be able to use it as a valid basis of comparison with other activities within and outside the group (such as the 2000 or so businesses in the Strategic Planning Institute data base).[1] If the profit is assessed after interest and investment income (and even more so after tax), the trend of performance is obscured by financing factors.

The following performance of a small US business with which we were involved is a case in point (see Table 3.2). If the activity profit and profit after tax are indexed to year 1, as shown in Fig. 3.1, the second index is much less an accurate measure of annual performance than the first because, as a result of pre-tax losses, virtually no tax is chargeable in year 2; and then the losses are carried forward to a period when reasonable profits are being made. In the same situation, more cash needs to be pumped into the business, incurring

Table 3.2

Year	1	2	3	4	5
	£m	£m	£m	£m	£m
Activity profit	1147	224	2028	2851	4030
Interest	(593)	(672)	(848)	(795)	(747)
Tax	(403)	(14)	(535)	(987)	(1598)
Profit after tax	151	(462)	645	1105	1685

higher interest. It will take a number of good years before the extra loans are paid off. During this period, major fluctuations in the interest rate also have a significant effect. It is irrelevant in the assessment of how well a business is doing, or can do, *in the market place* that it is funded by debt rather than equity, or that interest rates may be raised high because of government fiscal policies. So in this context, the best relative measure is profit pre-interest and tax. Tracing through to the final cash flow is a necessary part of the scenario planning process, but is dealt with at a later stage.

Arguments will always rage as to the propriety of allocating central costs to activities. On the one hand, failure to charge costs incurred centrally that are necessary for the proper running of a business means that the activity profit is overstated. Comparison with businesses outside the scope of such central charges becomes less valid. So the costs of divisional accounting or management may, for reasons of expediency, not be allocated, but the charge to the activity should be at least be ascertained. On the other hand, activity managers may be justified in complaining where excessive central costs, outside their control, are charged to them. In the event, the best solution is to show the appropriate amount of central charges as a separate item, without reducing activity profit. Senior management will then be able to review performance both in its own right and relative to other activities.

The remaining 'extraordinary' item is intended to cover those matters that are of a special non-recurring nature, whose inclusion in activity profit would result in a distortion in the time-series. If, for example, major restructuring has occurred, with write-offs and severance or redundancy payments to staff and so on, its inclusion might show a major change in profile.

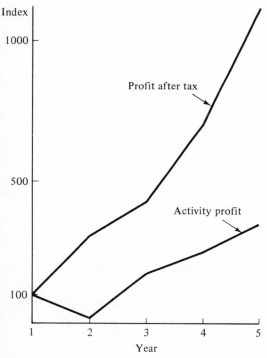

Figure 3.1 Comparing activity profit and profit after tax

The following example concerns another business that we recently reviewed (see Table 3.3). After a first, half-hearted, attempt to rationalize in year 2, a major shake-up in selling policies was introduced. The activity underwent major surgery in its distribution outlets, inventories and labour force. The graph of indices for the two profit lines (Fig. 3.2) shows that, not only are the absolute values markedly affected, but in two years out of the five, the direction of the profit trend is also changed by the extraordinary items. So the inclusion of exceptional factors that would obscure the trend in trading performance of the activity is avoided. They have to be stated, of course, and

Table 3.3

Year	1	2	3	4	5
	£m	£m	£m	£m	£m
Activity profit	11.4	15.3	14.3	16.1	20.3
Index	100	134	125	141	178
Extraordinary items	—	1.9	—	7.8	5.7
Adjusted profit	11.4	13.4	14.3	8.3	14.6
Index	100	118	125	73	128

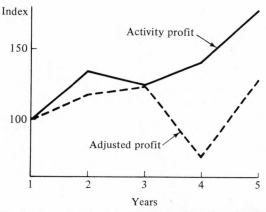

Figure 3.2 Comparing activity profit and profit after exceptional items

may represent most important factors in assessing the future of the business.
But they should be kept separate.

Working capital

The next item on the list, working capital, incorporates three items that
fluctuate seasonally, from month to month and even from day to day. In the
books it can even vary with the whims of the manager or accountant,
according to the impression they may wish to give over the short term. It is,
therefore, more usefully calculated for planning purposes on an average basis,
than as reported in the balance sheet. Fashion products, such as wallcoverings, have a major sales campaign in the spring, so that working capital will
peak with high inventories before that campaign. If the year end coincides
with the start of the campaign, an abnormally high working capital will
emerge which may give the unwarranted impression that this is a problem

area. Alternatively, a balance sheet struck during a period of low activity could perhaps hide undue profligacy, or a business that needs too much investment ever to be profitable.

For organizations that are in the early stages of development of their planning systems, the balance sheet approach is likely to be adopted for the sake of expediency, while managers become acquainted with the mechanics. It is always easier to use figures that reconcile with one another; but, more importantly, until management is convinced that those reporting to them are providing sufficiently accurate numbers in this area which can be very difficult to control, there is benefit in applying a rigorous accounting approach to reconciliation. Once there is a degree of maturity in operating the system, the more sophisticated average approach may be adopted. Whichever method is used, however, witch hunts in the guise of reconciliation must not be allowed to rule the planning round. The whole system will collapse if planners behave like an executive we know who insisted that any change in any item of

Table 3.4   Inventory changes in year 1980

		£
Opening inventories	100 units at £10	1000
Additions	120 units at £12	1440
Closing inventories	100 units at £12	(1200)
Charge to P & L a/c		1240

a plan had to be reconciled in all detail, including monthly phasing. A full computer program was written to enable this to be done, mounds of paper were produced, and the whole planning process ground to a halt as the objective of the staff became 'hunt the discrepancy'.

Inventories (or, more commonly in the UK, stocks) are, of course, an element of working capital. With inflation accelerating at a high rate, those companies that apply FIFO rules (first in first out) as used by most UK corporations for charging the P & L account will show a holding gain that is not reflected in cash flow. This means that, if the value of inventories charged is based on an earlier and lower cost than that of the inventories retained on the balance sheet, the effect is to enhance the profit by the difference in the value. The simple example in Table 3.4 will be familier to UK management, where the FIFO system has hitherto tended to be adopted. In this very simple example, the price of inventories inflates by 20 per cent. The P & L account is charged £200 less than the cost of inventories purchased during the year, so a holding gain of this amount emerges. This does not appear in the cash flow. For those organizations (commonly in the USA) using LIFO (last in first out) methods, so that the P & L account is charged the higher value of inventories, this problem does not arise, but there remains the question, in an inflationary environment, of the monetary working capital (MWC)—that is, the net value of receivables and payables.

This element of MWC varies significantly according to the type of business. Let us take three examples (Table 3.5). In the first case (A Bank Ltd), inflation will have an adverse impact on the value of MWC because the bank must keep a proportion of its assets in cash or cash equivalent. In the second (B Supermarket), since the business is run on a cash customer basis, there are virtually no debtors and inflation is beneficial in that it erodes the value of amounts owing to creditors. Finally, for the manufacturing company, the effect is minimal, as receivables and payables are more or less equal in value.[2]

A separate MWC value is not demanded, as it can be deduced from total working capital less inventories. It will therefore also be an average if averages

Table 3.5

	A Bank Ltd		B Supermarket Ltd		C Manufacturing Co Ltd	
		£m		£m		£m
Advances and liquid assets		1000	Customers	0	Trade debtors	30
Deposits received		(900)	Suppliers	(20)	Trade creditors	(28)
Net MWC		100		(20)		2

are used for the other items. It is not beyond the wit or will of managers, however, to obscure the overall working capital position by delaying payment of creditors or accelerating the payment of debts—even if, on occasion, at the expense of hefty discounts. Perhaps those companies that have had a bad experience should delve into this even more deeply so as to know on which side of MWC the damage is being done.

Fixed assets

In considering the few items relating to fixed assets, we admit that there may be some redundancy of information, in that:

- fixed assets at cost less fixed assets at net book amount = cumulative depreciation;
- cumulative depreciation year 2 less cumulative depreciation year 1 = depreciation in year 2;
- given a standard depreciation rate, R, then fixed assets at cost $\times R$ = depreciation for the year.

There are, however, adjustments normally to be made during the course of any year for capital expenditure and for asset disposal and also, though less frequently, for acquisition and disposal of businesses. A statement of all the items referred to on page 30 may, therefore, be necessary, and it will in all cases make life easier for the planners.

Just like working capital, so fixed assets are affected by inflation. It is now depressingly well-known that historic depreciation will rarely provide sufficent funds to maintain the profit-generating capacity of plant and equipment in real terms.[3] It is important, therefore, to know the amount in replacement depreciation (depreciation CCA) that would be needed for this purpose. Whether the activity will wish to spend up to this amount is, of course, dependent upon its chosen strategy—if it is expanding, it may spend more; if contracting, maybe less. The calculation of replacement depreciation is not a popular exercise among operating managers, but it forces a more rigorous appraisal of what plant and equipment is actually needed for the business and which parts will be replaced. The system of merely applying the retail price index to fixed assets at cost is altogether too crude to be useful. A paper-mill, for instance, may never need to replace the main frame of its paper-making machines, and the inflation index of paper-making machinery is unlikely to equate closely to the retail price index. The application of an unselective approach in this case, therefore, would probably indicate a replacement cost that would render the whole operation totally untenable. We know, however, that many papermakers do successfully refurbish and keep their mills up to scratch. So an uncritical and generalized approach to this problem can produce misleading answers which do a lot of damage: intellectual Luddites are lurking everywhere to throw hammers into valid concepts. They are presented with hammers to wreak their destruction every time a concept is applied in an inept way.

Non-financial information

We now move on to the non-financial information. The number of employees is self-explanatory and its use will be discussed later in the context of productivity in Chapter 7: it has already been mentioned in connection with the dynamics of labour costs in Chapter 1. The volume index is required to know how much of sales value change is attributable to volume of products sold and how much to price movement. This is important, and not just for the reasons mentioned in Chapter 2. Anticipating Chapter 7, we have created a dummy company, comprising various component activities. Detailed schedules of this corporation are included in Appendix 3. Looking at Schedule 5 of these, and assuming a single product (to eliminate mix), the pattern of price increases can be calculated (Table 3.6).

37

Table 3.6

	1975	1976	1977	1978	1979	1980	1981	1982
Volume index	75	85	84	90	96	100	104	108
Price index	62	68	73	76	87	100	109	117

In this particular case, volume growth stalled in 1977. Prices rose just over 10 per cent in 1976 and somewhat less in 1977 and 1978, but both volume and price contributed to a boom in 1979. The years thereafter are forecasts, and the immediate question that the time-series raises is: will the buoyancy be sustained so that the business achieves both a 4 per cent volume growth and a 15 per cent price rise in 1980?

The above example was simplified by eliminating any question of product mix. This is a complex matter. A volume index that aggregates a mix of products can be calculated by one of the formulae:

$$(1) \quad \frac{\sum_{i=1}^{n} P_{0i} Q_{1i}}{\sum_{i=1}^{n} P_{0i} Q_{0i}}$$

or

$$(2) \quad \frac{\sum_{i=1}^{n} P_{1i} Q_{1i}}{\sum_{i=1}^{n} P_{1i} Q_{0i}}$$

where

P is price
Q is quantity sold
0 is base year
1 is end year
$\sum_{i=1}^{n}$ is sum of i items, 1 to n.

Equation (1), known as Laspeyres index, calculates the volume index using constant prices for the base year to aggregate the quantities. Equation (2), the Paasche index, uses end-period price weights. Each is equally valid, but they are likely to produce different results.[4] Between the base and end year the relative prices of the products may well have changed, and, as a consequence, perhaps more of the relatively cheaper items are bought. Considerable divergencies could result: as one statistician was fond of saying, 'It pays to know your Paasche from your Laspeyres.'

Indices have other dangerous properties. First, the mix may not remain constant; the products may increase or reduce in number, or be replaced. This introduces a discontinuity. Second, though the product may remain the same (e.g., a litre can of white emulsion paint), the technical qualities may improve substantially (e.g., the paint has far greater covering power)—another discontinuity. These problems apply equally to price indices. Yet everybody seems content to use nationally constructed rates of inflation, where all these problems are multiplied, so perhaps too much should not be made of the difficulties—except to warn the user that, in our experience, this is a fertile ground for dissension.

In any event, many problems are avoided by considering the objectives for gleaning the information. Common sense will help. If mix changes are not major and permanent, it is probably unnecessary to delve further: ignore them. The price-plus-mix factor will adequately show how much more money the business is trying to take out of the market place for given volumes of product. If the tactics are, however, to move up or down market in a significant, long-term way during the process of change, more detailed information should be required to illuminate what is planned. In major cases it may be necessary to separate the activity into its individual products—in line with the 'business units' philosophy set out in Chapter 2.

Another useful feature of the volume index is that it enables a rough check on the capital expenditure–capacity utilization relationship. Schedule 5 also illustrates how, as sales volumes have risen, so has production as measured by capacity utilization (though they do not march precisely in step). Capacity utilization in the first plan year (1980) is, however, expected to exceed 100 per cent of standard capacity, that is to say, the figures adopted by management as the rate of production that the plant may normally be expected to sustain. This figure can, of course, be exceeded for short bursts. This was true, for example, of our own corporation's paper mills in 1973. If however, the volumes projected show a long-term need in excess of standard capacity, capital expenditure has to rise to meet this. As a broad guide, it should show an amount in excess of the simple cost of replacement while production capability is built up. Note that, in accountancy terms, the cost of replacement is shown as replacement or CCA depreciation. The detail is extracted in Table 3.7. The picture is one of a business where the management has its capital investment reasonably well balanced against its market strategy.

Financial consolidation

Having looked at the basic building blocks of the system—the component activities—the next consideration is the information needed to put it all

Table 3.7

	1975	1976	1977	1978	1979	1980	1981	1982
Volume index (1980=100)	75	85	84	90	96	100	104	108
Capacity utilization (%)	76	83	86	94	100	102	97	95
Capital expenditure (£m) exceeds/falls short of replacement cost	(0.2)	(0.2)	(0.1)	0.1	0.2	0.2	—	(0.2)

together in a consolidated plan. In a highly automated system subsidiary consolidations may be avoided. In practice, however, for the better management of sets of similar activities, most corporations will gather such activities into divisions.

If so, plan consolidations are prepared at each divisional level to facilitate the planning process and to enable divisional managers to control the totality of their operations. These subsidiary consolidations will then be used to create the full group consolidation, but it must be recognized that, while they are useful to assist in the accounting work of planning and in the subsequent monitoring of divisional managers' performance, the numbers in the subsidiary consolidation have no real significance in scenario planning.

The corporate figures are prepared in the usual form of:

• profit and loss account
• balance sheet
• cash flow statement

Completed examples are included in Appendix 3. Of these schedules, the last is the most important for scenario planning, as all changes are calculated at the cash flow level and expressed as differences on annual or cumulative cash flows. The type of statement required in its simplest form is shown in Table 3.8. This statement is basically divided into two parts:

• the operational elements, which include the first nine items
• the financing elements, which are the remainder

The merits of separating operating and financing items have already been discussed. Acquisitions and disposals are included above the financing line, because these are treated as normal factors in the long-term running of a business. They are undertaken not to manipulate the finances of the business, but to consolidate or reduce the activity's presence in the market. If, indeed, certain assets are held for non-operational reasons, and form part of the central pool of resource for funding the group, they should not be held at divisional

Table 3.8

| | | Actual | | Original Estimate [plan] [as at] | | Plan | | |
		1977	1978	1979	1979	1980	1981	1982
		(1)	(2)	(3)	(4)	(5)	(6)	(7)
Trading profit	(1)							
Depreciation	(2)							
Inflow from trading	(3)							
Capital expenditure	(4)							
Working capital movement	(5)							
Trading cash flow	(6)							
Acquisitions	(7)							
Disposals	(8)							
Cash flow before financing	(9)							
Net group interest	(10)							
Dividends payable	(11)							
Taxation	(12)							
Total cash flow	(13)							
Opening borrowings	(14)							
Long-term movement	(15)							
Short-term movement	(16)							
Closing borrowings	(17)							

level, except for legal or political reasons. In any organization the concept that any part of the liquid resource 'belongs' exclusively to a division or other component unit (except, as stated, in a strictly legal sense) has no place. The concept is often held strongly in businesses that are being harvested as part of the group strategy. 'We produce the cash,' they say, 'so we must be allowed to use it.' The resource in fact has to be used in order to optimize the corporate objective as a whole, and if another activity can use it to produce better returns, that other activity gets it.

The balance sheet is, of course, also important in creating the group plan. One of the chief constraints upon a corporation's growth opportunities is the limitation imposed upon its borrowing powers, by the policy adopted on debt–equity ratio. The debt–equity figure needs to be ascertained for different courses of action in different economic scenarios to test whether the constraint is broken. Our own corporation was particularly aware of the problem when, in the late 1970s, following a series of inadequately profitable acquisitions and

41

mismatched currency exposures, the debt–equity ratio rose to around 200 per cent. Corporate thinking was concentrated on getting this down to manageable levels. Various programmes for disposal, restructuring, and good housekeeping were proposed and considered within a policy of rapid de-escalation of the gearing. In the event, the course adopted resulted within three years in a significantly enhanced return on investment, a trading profit maintained in absolute terms and with much reduced interest charges, and a drop in the debt–equity ratio to below 50 per cent.

If, however, each business had been permitted to go its own way as best it could, the debt–equity ratio, already high, would have risen to heights where only an astronomical observatory could have continued to track it.

This completes the description of the structure and scope of the hub of the system. The data-base itself largely comprises the financial information that describes the structure of the business, while the models incorporate the dynamics. The next step is to look at the linkages that connect the hub to events in the universe.

Notes

1. For a review of the use of the PIMS data base for comparative purposes, see the report on *DROLA (Dynamic Report on 'Look-Alikes')*, Strategic Planning Institute, Boston, 1980.
2. A simplified version of the detail given in *Current Cost Accounting* (ED 24), Accounting Standards Committee, London, April 1979, footnote at end of Preface.
3. See, for the whole subject of current cost accounting, Mallison, *Understanding CCA*, Butterworths, London, 1980.
4. F. E. Croxton, D. J. Cowden, and S. Klein, *Applied General Statistics*, 3rd edn, Pitman, London, 1968, chs. 17 and 18.

4.
Linkages

The nature of linkages

The stock exchanges of the world must be the envy of all roller-coaster manufacturers. They seem capable of engineering rises and falls of such breath-taking proportions, with the most meagre materials, that it leaves onlookers awe-struck and shareholders with butterflies in the stomach. The speed with which political and economic developments are discounted in the bond and share markets may not at first sight seem to have any basis in rationality; it is, after all, a market in which 'sentiment' plays a major rôle. The object is to guess what's happening ahead of the competitors—the other brokers and jobbers. So calculations are being made and hunches played at breakneck speed on how the profitability of a company will be affected by the latest political or economic snippet. A significant feature, though, is their recognition that the economic climate in which companies operate does, in fact, affect profitability greatly.

Fortunately for most firms, ill winds take longer to blow through than the speed with which the stock exchanges discount them. The scenario-builder has to adopt a more cautious and scientific approach. He must be precise about the transmission mechanisms between the macroeconomic environment and his businesses with respect to both speed and magnitude. A chief executive will not be satisfied with the bland assessment proferred by a stockbroker to his bemused client that 'market sentiment' has turned against his shares. He will need to be persuaded of the chain of causation. And the words of the scenario-planner will carry conviction only if he is clear himself about the relationship between one link and the next.

The terms 'link' or 'linkages' are now used in a special sense. The earlier concept of a spoke in a wheel has to be developed to one of a transmission belt between the external environment and the activity's performance. They perform a dynamic, rather than purely static, function and we now go into this in depth. Chapter 2 explained how a company's performance can be gauged from the conventional set of accounting identities, which we call the financial model. A linkage has one end firmly attached to the accounting variables; the other infiltrates that nebulous space termed the 'external environment', over which business managers have very little control or influence (see Fig. 4.1).

This is not to suggest that only single links can be devised between the two. In fact, the chain is invariably longer, often passing, as was described, from the macroeconomic environment through the markets in which the company participates and thence to the corporation.

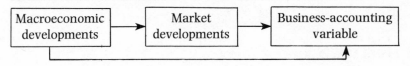

Figure 4.1 From the environment to the business

Economy to markets

Probing the space around the immediate confines of the managerial responsibility, an activity can be seen to participate in at least four supply-side markets, as well as that into which it is selling.
These are:

- the labour market
- the raw materials and energy market
- the capital goods market
- the financial market

Turbulence in any one of these is likely to have repercussions for the activity. The scenario-planner is in the business of 'what sort of turbulence' and 'what kind of repercussions'. Since he is interested in quantifiable aspects, the market linkages must be capable of taking developments in the economy and translating them into such market parameters as price, domestic sales, exports, etc. The linkage must, furthermore, have a time dimension. An external shock may come through to the market quickly or very slowly; it is important to know which, and the linkage should be able to help in this respect.

It is this last feature that most clearly distinguishes linkages from trends. The objective in using the latter is to come to conclusions about the direction over time in which a particular series is moving, whereas a linkage wishes to project, as closely as may be, the specific movement in each time period that that series will take. Figure 4.2 illustrates the point. The solid line shows some profits for a hypothetical corporation. The *trend* of those profits is given by the dotted line—the best fit was calculated on an exponential basis. Since our objective was to assist managers with short- to mid-term movements about the trend, we had to do better than this and actually produce a curve that would fit the past and project a more detailed future. It would have been no consolation to the manager of that business to know his forecasts were on trend if he had gone out of business in 1967 or 1974 through failure to recognize the cyclicality of his profit and cash flow.

We have seen how, at the accounting end of linkages, both the labour and raw materials' markets represent sources of current costs. The scenario-planners' interest in these is limited to the price of his corporation's products and more particularly of those his component activities consume in any

44

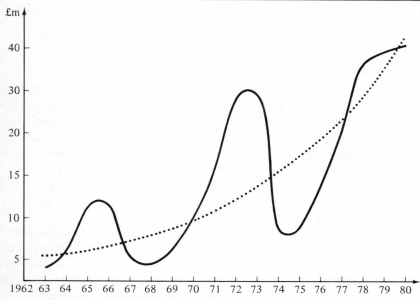

Figure 4.2 Cycles and trends

quantity. Once he has identified the principal items, he needs to build an analytical structure that adequately explains movements in costs.

A cost model would also be needed, for gauging the price of capital goods appropriate for investment in the business. These costs would obviously have their impact on balance sheet items, whereas movements in financial markets can affect both the P & L account and the balance sheet. For instance, a rise in interest rates is likely to result, all else being equal, in reduced profits, as the cost of servicing past borrowings rises. In this case an interest rate model would be required by the scenario-planner. Similarly, movements in the exchange rate, besides having direct consequences for perhaps both costs and revenue, can also bear importantly on balance sheet items. A UK company may have borrowed heavily from foreign banks to finance development and will show its debt in sterling. If sterling depreciates against other currencies, the size of that debt grows in domestic terms. So in such cases an exchange rate model is needed also.

Finally, the scenario-planner needs to explain movements in the markets into which his company is selling. Geographically, the markets may span both domestic and foreign economies, and he will be looking for models capable of explaining movements in both sales volume and price. Although from a purely accounting point of view, only sales revenue is required, we have seen how many features of company behaviour depend critically on volume. So taking

45

all these factors into consideration, we are now in a position to start building specific models.

Designing models

So far, we have thought of models as analytical structures without being too precise. Formal definitions are not very helpful, so the description that follows really echoes the sentiment of the man who once remarked, 'I can't define an elephant, but I know one when I see one.' We are going to define models by their more obvious attributes. As a start, we may say that mathematical models contain equations that seek to explain the values of certain variables, given the values of others.

Straightforwardly, if $x = 1$, then $y = 2$; if GDP movement $= -3$ per cent, then unemployment $= 2.5$ million (say).

The variables explained by a model are termed endogenous (output) variables while the variables that are a prerequisite for the functioning of the model are called exogenous (input) variables.[1] The type of equation under consideration is sometimes called 'behavioural', since it tells the user about the behaviour of the output variable, given assumptions about the input terms. Behavioural equations stand apart from 'identities', which are essentially accounting definitions. For instance, sales value for a single product is, by definition, a product of price and volume. There could be a model with two behavioural equations for price and volume and an accounting identity to establish sales value.

The simplest model is a one-equation model in which the output variable is explained by a single input variable. For instance, the cost of labour in the markets where a company bids may be so closely related to the UK average earnings index that a scenario-planner may opt to use the following:

$$W_t = a + b_1 E_t \qquad (4.1)$$

where:

W_t is a market wage index in time period t

E is the UK average earnings index in time period t

b_1 is the coefficient relating the two indices

a is a constant

In this equation W is the output term and E the input variable. The coefficients a and b are calculated by using a technique known as ordinary least squares, or, as it is sometimes called, simple bivariate regression.[2] (A discussion of techniques is included in Appendix 4.) It is, of course, possible to expand the single-equation model to include many more exogenous terms. For instance, theory, or simple business insight, might indicate that price in a market is determined by a simple mark-up on raw material prices and labour costs; thus

$$P_t = a + b_1 W_t + b_2 R_t \qquad (4.2)$$

where, adopting the same notation as the previous equation, of the new variables, P_t is the market price of a business product in period t and R_t is the cost of raw materials in period t. With sufficient data on P, W, and R, multiple regression can be used to estimate the cofficients b_1 and b_2 (see Appendix 4.)[3] The techniques for estimation involve a lot of number-crunching, but fortunately computers remove much of the toil. Most time-sharing systems will have statistical packages that will do the necessary calculations.

Although it is comforting to know that a computer chip will do in a fraction of a second calculations that by hand would have taken hours, there are attendant dangers. In the past, the physical effort and time involved in statistical manipulation was onerous enough to ensure that the theory was thought through before tests were run. Nowadays, with the power of computers, it is very tempting to adopt a 'suck-it-and-see' attitude. This should be resisted. Scenario planning is the quantification of the consequences flowing from changed assumptions about the future. Its purpose is to permit executives to take timely measures, some of which may seem at the time very stringent. Communicating the story of a scenario through its various linkages is essential to the process. If the planner takes refuge in mathematical mystification he will lose not only his audience, but his objective. When formulating relationships between market variables and the environment, therefore, it is essential to start with a theoretical or *a priori* argument that produces a testable hypothesis.[4] The statistical analysis is merely a test of the hypothesis, and one that must necessarily provide only grounds for rejection. In this as in any other sphere, it is not possible to *prove* that a theory holds, but merely to prove that it is consistent with the known facts. If, therefore, the modeller starts with a postulated relationship that from experience and cogent argument seems valid and, furthermore, is consistent with available information, he has a linkage that will be comprehensible and bear scrutiny.

The following sections describe econometric model-building techniques needed not just for market linkages, but also for the macroeconomic relationships used in the models described in Chapter 5. The emphasis is on the concepts, rather than a detailed description of the techniques themselves, so that non-econometricians may follow and assess the validity of the approach. The manager concerned to know more about planning may thereby acquire sufficient 'specialist' knowledge to cope sympathetically with the problems (and sternly with the 'try-ons') of a multi-disciplinary team. Appendix 4 delves into greater detail, though it continues in the language of the layman wherever possible. Occasionally technical terms are used, because they form part of the econometrician's daily vocabulary, and it is as well to understand the key terms. If the departmental econometrician approaches the manager complaining that he has a homoscedastic problem, the manager who has read Appendix 4 will at least know whether to recommend a visit to the company psychiatrist, hold a meeting with the company lawyer present, or suggest a Spearman's Rank Correlation test!

The random element

Sceptics usually explode at the point where it is suggested that the complexity of the market can be caught by a theoretically specified equation. Much of the opposition is based on a misconception of the nature of the exercise, which in turn may be due to too much overselling of the idea by the modeller. The theoretical specification is an attempt to isolate those forces that explain the movement in a given variable. Yet the sceptics have a point, for clearly the relationships between the macroeconomic environment and the market (as captured by available data) are far too complex, and subject to too many vagaries, to be entirely systematic. Furthermore, it will be inevitable that the data used will be limited and, therefore, will represent only a sample observation which may contain biases. Under these circumstances, it is not a realistic possibility to develop exact equations which completely explain the movements of a given variable.

On the other hand, it is unreasonable to suggest that demand, supply, and price are entirely randomly determined—if they were, managerial 'experience' would not be worth a candle: it would consist of a series of incoherent and unrepeatable events and attempts to manage on the basis of experience would fail. As specified, equations (4.1) and (4.2) above are, in fact, exact equations. Since any pretension to such precision is fanciful, they need to be respecified. Economic relationships, therefore, can be seen as embracing two elements; one systematic, derivable from theory, and the other, a random element, representing the difference between the systematic and the real world.

Equation (4.1) should therefore be rewritten thus:

$$W_t = a + b_1 E_t + e_t \qquad (4.3)$$

where e_t is this random term. It is in fact the residual between the systematic element $\hat{W}_t$ given by $a + b_1 E_t$ and the real world values W_t:

$$W_t - \hat{W}_t = e_t. \qquad (4.4)$$

Although it is not possible to conclude anything about the values of the error terms since they are random, a great deal can be done to reduce uncertainty if assumptions are made about the probability of their occurrence. This might seem an even tougher requirement, but, in fact, it is not necessarily so. If a card were to be drawn at random from a bridge pack, its face value might not be known, but the probability of a given card's being drawn must be 1/52. The probability of a face card is 12/52 and of an ace, 4/52. Statisticians, using generalized probability distributions, have devised techniques that allow the inference of coefficients of equations for the real world. Thus the techniques for

48

devising equations depend on specific assumptions about the general nature of the probability distribution. These equations, containing an error term with a given distribution, are termed 'stochastic'.

Nonlinear equations

So far, models have been discussed in terms of single stochastic linear equations whose coefficients are determined by regression analysis. There is no reason why economic relationships need be linear, and the availability of linear estimating techniques should not seduce the planner to mis-specify the model in linear terms. There are reasonably sophisticated nonlinear techniques described in advanced textbooks and available on many computer packages.[5] There are, however, much simpler devices, such as logarithms, to convert a nonlinear to a linear equation.

Imagine a scatter diagram (as for example is contained in Appendix 4) of market wages, W_t, and UK average earnings, E_t, which shows that a unit increase in E_t seems accompanied by a fixed 'proportional' increase in W_t (i.e., it yields a curve). By taking logarithms of W_t the curve may be straightened; the equations would assume the following linear log form:

$$\log W_t = \log a + \log bE_t. \tag{4.5}$$

The cofficients $\log a$ and $\log b$ could then be estimated using regression. Taking antilogs of both sides would yield the nonlinear form:

$$W_t = ab^{E_t} \tag{4.6}$$

The modeller might, however, feel that the curvature would not be removed by taking logs of just W_t but that a log form of E_t is also needed. This would give the following:

$$\log W_t = \log a + b \log E_t \tag{4.7}$$

which would permit ordinary least square estimation of logs a and b. This gives the nonlinear equation:

$$W_t = a\, E_t^b. \tag{4.8}$$

The double-log transformation given above is often used in demand equations since it yields directly the price elasticity of demand. Other transformations include taking the reciprocal of either the dependent variable $(1/W_t)$ or the independent variable $(1/E_t)$. Alternatively, the modeller might feel that the relationship follows some polynomial form, e.g.:

$$W_t = a + bE_t + cE_t^2 \text{ (second degree)} \tag{4.9}$$
or
$$W_t = a + bE_t + cE_t^2 + dE_t^3 \text{ (third degree)}. \tag{4.10}$$

Provided the data are suitably transformed for the regression calculation, there is no difficulty in ascertaining the coefficient.

49

A word of warning: econometricians have been known to lunge into exotic equation forms in a desperate attempt to improve the explanatory power of the exogenous variables. The various nonlinear equations mentioned have specific characteristics, depending on the values of the coefficients, and it is advisable to decide whether these properties have a valid common-sense meaning before finally accepting them.

Recursive models

So far, models have been discussed in terms of single, linear, or nonlinear equations, with either one or more exogenous variables explaining the systematic movement in the endogenous series. Quite often, however, more complex models are needed. Consider this simple set of equations and identities which describe various aspects of the consumer magazine market:

$$P_m = f(\bar{E}, \bar{P}_p) \tag{4.11}$$

$$C_m = f(P_m/\bar{P}_0, \bar{C}) \tag{4.12}$$

$$S_m = P_m \times C_m \tag{4.13}$$

where:
P_m is the cover price of magazines
E is the wage costs in the economy
P_p is the cost of printing paper
C_m is the volume consumption of magazines
P_0 is the consumer price index
C is aggregate consumption in the economy
S_m is the magazine sales value

(The bars over certain symbols denote that the variables they represent are exogenous.) In theoretical terms it is saying that magazine publishers, be it via oligopoly, market leadership, or whatever, are in a position to operate a simple mark-up on wage and paper prices to set magazine prices. The level of demand, C_m, is not relevant to price. The price equation, P_m, is determined by entirely input variables. Wage costs may have come from a macroeconomic forecast or scenario simulation. Paper costs are provided by assumption. Since the equation for P_m is independent of the equation for C_m, it is possible to estimate it first and then feed the values into the consumption equation. The consumption of magazines is seen to be a function of the relative price of magazines, that is, relative to the consumer price index, and the aggregate level of consumption. The input terms can be found from macroeconomic forecasts. The values from the price and consumption equations can now feed into the identity for sales value, S_m.

This type of model is termed 'recursive' because of the characteristics that allow the results of one equation to feed into the other. There is a one-way causal chain. Although this system has great appeal, because the arguments of cause and effect are readily appreciated and explained to others, it is not always possible to isolate cause from effect so crisply.

Simultaneous models

The equation systems mentioned hitherto have been in terms of self-contained equations, standing by themselves or feeding into others as exogenous terms. Consider the following two equations:

$$P = a + bC + cR \qquad b > 0, \quad c < 0 \qquad\qquad (4.14)$$

$$R = d + eP + fB \qquad e < 0, \quad f > 0 \qquad\qquad (4.15)$$

where P is the cover price of a national newspaper, C is its unit costs, R the advertising rate, and B, cash balances of corporations.

These equations express the following theoretical view of pricing newspapers and advertising: cover price will increase with production costs but reduce as a result of advertising income; advertising rates, on the other hand, rise when corporations have plenty of cash but fall if cover prices are buoyant. The two behavioural equations might be termed 'structural equations', since they lay out the theoretical structure of the model. However, the value of P is dependent on R, while at the same time R is dependent on P. It is obviously necessary to capture this interactive quality when estimating the coefficients. Independent estimation could produce biased and inconsistent results. Fortunately, with a little algebra it is possible to rearrange the equations so that the simultaneous characteristics of the model can be expressed in terms of input variables C and B.

Substituting equation (4.15) into equation (4.14), we get for cover price

$$P = a + BC + c(d + eP + fB) \qquad\qquad (4.16)$$

$$P = \frac{a + cd}{1 - ce} + \frac{b}{1 - ce} C + \frac{cf}{1 - ce} B \qquad\qquad (4.17)$$

$$P = K_1 + S_1 C + S_2 B. \qquad\qquad (4.18)$$

The price equation is now expressed in terms of a constant $K_1 = (a + cd)/(1 - ce)$; the slope coefficient on costs, $S_1 = b/(1 - ce)$; and on cash balances, $S_2 = cf/(1 - ce)$. This new version of the equation is termed the 'reduced form', to denote that the interactive characteristics of the structural equations containing output terms on the right-hand side have been reduced to a simple dependence on the input terms only. Using least squares techniques, both slope coefficients and the constant can be estimated. This process of finding the reduced form first and then using least squares is sometimes called 'indirect least squares'.

51

Substituting the reduced form of the cover price equation into the structural form of the advertising equation results in:

$$R = d + e\left(\frac{a+cd}{1-ce} + \frac{b}{1-ce}C + \frac{cf}{1-ce}B\right) + fB \tag{S}$$

$$R = d + \frac{e(a+cd)}{1-ce} + \frac{eb}{1-ce}C + \frac{ecf}{1-ce} + fB \tag{T}$$

$$R = K_2 + S_3C + S_4B. \tag{U}$$

The only restriction on a simultaneous system is that there should be at least as many equations as unknown output terms. This is merely a necessary condition for algebraic solution. Once again, the slope coefficient and the constant can be found by least squares and the direct and indirect effects, captured accurately.

Identification

When estimating coefficients it is important to check not only that their values do not imply an absurdity but that their signs conform with theoretical expectations. In the consumer magazine example, there are four slope estimates, $S1$, $S2$, $S3$, and $S4$. Can there be any certainty, however, that the signs expected on b, c, e, and f are fulfilled? Fortunately, there are four equations for each slope in the four unknown structural coefficients, so it is possible to solve for b, c, e, and f. In these circumstances the model is said to be identified because the structural coefficients can be found.

Quite often, however, it is not possible to identify fully the structural coefficients: perhaps only one or two can be found. The under-identification may be enough to establish that the remaining coefficients either have or do not have the correct sign. All the same, in the absence of knowledge about the structural coefficients, it is not possible to measure the direct impact of a change in an input variable on the output variable. Policy-making often requires this sort of information, but for scenario planning there is not over-much concern that the direct and indirect effects of a change are merged into one coefficient since interest is centred on the net effect of a change. So under-identification need not present too many difficulties; over-identification, however, raises estimation problems.

Over-identification arises when it is possible to solve for a structural coefficient in more than one way, so that there are at least two possible values for it. Under these circumstances ordinary least squares is not a suitable technique, and a method such as two-stage least squares should be adopted. Although there is no need to describe in detail the nature of the calculation, in principle it works as follows: the first equation is estimated, as normal, against the input terms, and the disturbance term is isolated; then it is substracted from the actual values of the first output series and the resultant systematic value is fed into the second equation for estimation of the coefficients. In this way the bias and lack of consistency in one-stage least squares is removed.

Statistical packages

Much of the number-crunching involved in finding equations and building models is available on computer time-sharing systems and micro-computer packages. What general features are required of any software package? The problems of model-building are quite sufficient, without the extra headaches of persuading a computer to do what is wanted by excessively long and tortuous devices. The first requirement of any system is, therefore, simplicity in use. Unfortunately, the simpler it is to use, the more intricate must be the programming and, consequently, the more expensive.

The second requirement is that good, well documented macroeconomic data bases should be readily available to, and directly accessible by, the statistical program. Normally the modeller will provide his own data in the specific markets that he is trying to model and this alone can be very time-consuming. If all the necessary macroeconomic data have to be collected and regularly updated as well, there would be precious little time left for the model-building. The third general requirement is that there should be facilities for the modeller to catalogue his own data. Frequently data will be loaded into the system and given a user-specified name—a short mnemonic—for subsequent reference. Furthermore, these data may subsequently be trans-formed into percentage changes, logarithms, or first differences and stored for future use. In short, data bases tend to grow, with the consequent danger that, in the absence of a cataloguing system, the mnemonics fail to stimulate the memory and the planner is left wondering what on earth the data mean. A cataloguing system should have at least four attributes attached to the user defined mnemonic:

- time-span of the series
- title of the series
- source of data
- when last updated

The knowledge of these attributes allows the system user to keep a tidy house and not become swamped with meaningless variable names.

In addition to these general requirements, there are certain minimum features that the package must provide:

- data transformation, i.e., percentage change, logarithms, first differences
- mathematical functions $+$, $-$, $\div$, $\times$, raising to powers and taking roots
- data display, graphing, and tabling routines

53

- ordinary least squares with test statistics (see Appendix 4)
- auto-regressive transforms (see Appendix 4)
- two-stage least squares
- model-solving packages

Most statistical packages provide these as a matter of course and generally a good deal more. However, these items represent the absolute minima for building the sort of models that would be used in scenario planning.

Having estimated an equation or a set of equations, a convenient mechanism must be designed for combining them to project future values for all the output variables. The input data must be provided for future years and must be fed into the equations. If there is just one equation or the model is recursive, the problem is relatively trivial and is coped with most easily. However, if the system consists of a series of simultaneous equations or, indeed, if only a part of it contains identified structural equations of this sort, something a good deal more sophisticated is required. Various computing techniques are available for solving this sort of simultaneous equation and go by the names of their designers. Perhaps the one most commonly used is the Gauss–Seidel technique, but there are others too—Newton–Raphson and Fletcher–Powell.[6] It is merely coincidence that two mathematicians seem to be needed to crack these particular nuts, and it is in no way a measure of the complexity of the problem.

Manipulating endogenous and residual terms

Although the means to solve equations on the basis of input variables is a necessary attribute, it is not sufficient for a useful tool: other features are also required. If the model is to be used for forecasting, or indeed if market scenarios are to be based on the model, then it is essential to have some means of directly influencing the output variables. The fitted equations are stochastic and have an error term in their estimation. So when forecasting, values must be found for the error terms over the forecast period. Either they can be held at the last level they achieved, or some thought could go into sculpting their future profile. For instance, a major strike recently depressed market sales in one of our businesses. The equation forecasting sales of the activity calculated a higher level than actually occurred. This must happen unless there had been a specific term to take account of strikes and this was correctly anticipated. The latest residual, in the event, was large and negative, and it would seem unreasonable to suppose that it would stay at that level; so future residuals needed to be adjusted.

Alternatively, there might be detected in the residuals' tendencies to move in sympathy with other variables in the model. For instance, the residual on exports of a particular product might be moving inversely with the pressure of domestic demand, suggesting that domestic producers treat exports as an overflow tank. This would indicate mis-specification in the model. Although re-estimation to take account of this relationship would be best, in the meantime an appropriate judgement could be applied to the residual.

Residuals can also be manipulated to generate market scenarios. In addition to making alternative assumptions about the input values, residuals on output variables can be manipulated to simulate a desired effect. Suppose it were anticipated that the Chancellor might introduce a new tax on a particular product. The model-user could show this as a price rise, an upward adjustment to the price residual which would then feed into the volume equations showing the consequences for sales revenue. The ability to adjust output variables via the residual is, therefore, a most useful tool; it permits extra-model judgement and analysis to be fed into the model so that it becomes less of a black box and far more of a tool that interacts with human judgement and experience.

As residuals can play an important rôle in the running of models, it is important to monitor the individual track record of each component equation. This amounts to tracking the residual. Some model-solving packages permit the user to fix newly released actual values for the output variables and, given the correct actual values for the output variables, to work out the residual. So, when new data for the input variables are released, the current residuals can be readily calculated and compared with past values. From this sort of exercise can be detected whether the validity of an equation is tending to break down or not.

A final feature that can be of use to a modeller is a facility to exogenize an output variable. With simultaneous systems and time-lags it is not always an easy matter to make residual changes that would adequately simulate a desired effect or scenario. It is sometimes easier to fix an output variable at a specific value for a certain future date, perhaps to reflect a price freeze, and then allow the model to solve for other values of the system given that constraint.

Gauging market vulnerabilities

Once a battery of models has been built that reflect the environment in which a corporation operates, a fairly sharp picture of the types of economic variables in which the company as a whole is dependent becomes apparent. A company may find that many of its activities are in markets vulnerable to levels of, say, consumer expenditure or private investment. Equally, they may be in markets very sensitive to import penetration, and the level of domestic competitiveness assumes some importance. This qualitative information can be very useful in aiding the design of scenarios. With a knowledge of peculiar dependencies, and using economic theory, scenarios can be devised that will significantly shift those areas of dependence. This theme will be discussed more fully in the subsequent chapters.

Notes

1. E. J. Kane, *Economic Statistics and Econometrics: An Introduction to Quantitative Economics*, Harper & Row, New York, 1968, ch. 2.
2. For a simple explanation see K. A. Yeomans, *Introducing Statistics* (*Statistics for the Social Scientist*, vol. I), Penguin, Harmondsworth, 1968, ch. 5.
3. For a simple explanation see K. A. Yeomans, *Applied Statistics* (*Statistics for the Social Scientist*, vol. II), Penguin, Harmondsworth, 1968, ch. 4.
4. For a succinct defence of this positivism in economics, see R. G. Lipsey, *An Introduction to Positive Economics*, Weidenfeld & Nicolson, London, 1968, ch. 1.
5. C. F. Christ, *Econometric Models and Methods*, John Wiley, New York, 1966, pp. 432–52.
6. L. R. Klein and R. M. Young, *An Introduction to Econometric Forecasting and Forecasting Models*, Lexington Books, D. C. Heath & Co., Toronto, 1980, pp. 61–7.

5.
Macroeconomic models

We now have our models, like musical instruments, just needing to be blended into a unified sound. The financial model must be supplied with future macroeconomic values such as exchange rates (for consolidation purposes) and interest rates (for debt calculations). It also needs the microeconomic market projections for both revenue and cost components. These, in turn, require future macroeconomic inputs—consumer spending, retail prices, and so on. The macrovariables, therefore, become the common factors that unify the system. However, these macroeconomic variables have to be consistent, both internally and with the postulated scenario. Consistency is central to the theme of scenario planning, and we come back to this point shortly. What we need, therefore, to orchestrate the models is a mechanism that will generate future macroeconomic values consistent with a scenario—namely, a macroeconomic model.

Macroeconomic models are most commonly encountered in the preparation of forecasts to be used as the basis for plans and hence action.[1] Forecasts are, in fact, the highest probability scenario; lower probability developments can also be simulated. These models are conceptually similar to the simultaneous models described in the previous chapter. They, too, consist of simultaneous equations and identities, usually a very large number, that predict the output variables from inputs.

In size, they are to the market models what Notre Dame is to a wayside shrine. They must, therefore, be computer-based, and the solution methods normally used involve iterative techniques. That is to say, the computer will plug in one set of values for all the output variables to see how close it comes to meeting the solution criteria. If the solution criteria are not met, the computer will make some small changes to the previous plug-in values and try again, until it converges on a mathematically acceptable set of solution values. This iterative process can become very expensive on a time-sharing system, especially when the model is large and is being asked to look many years ahead. Furthermore, convergence is not always guaranteed. Occasionally models fail to converge because particular equations may be unstable over certain ranges or, alternatively, because the types of adjustments made may be probing into realms where the model cannot cope.

If macro-models are so expensive to use, do they justify this cost? In principle, future values could be assumed for the input terms in the market models. If consumer expenditure were an important variable in a market model, a set of values could be plugged in, bracketing the current forecast. But this is inadequate. What price and wage assumptions would be consistent with the assumed range of consumer expenditure? The *general* level of prices and wages would, furthermore, have some bearing on those experienced by the business, and these would also have an important influence on company profitability. Depressed consumer demand might arise from a temporary decline in average earnings relative to prices. Thus, although lower sales volume from reduced consumer expenditure might adversely affect margins, there could well be gains from the favourable movement in cost structures. So in estimating macroeconomic variables, it is no use snatching at random numbers: the structure must be coherent or it is valueless.

Macro-models, therefore, offer the necessary consistency. This is a key point underlying the entire approach to scenario planning. If an economic scenario is simulated on a macro-model, the future values of numerous output terms corresponding to input terms in market models will be internally consistent, because they fall within a common behavioural structure. The swings and roundabouts of the economy are thus reproduced in a structurally coherent way and transmitted via the market models to the business.

Executives must have reflected from time to time that, while profits sagged in one area of a corporation's business, they were fortunately offset by a better-than-expected performance elsewhere. Is it purely good fortune, or is it that, if the economic fabric of capitalist societies is strained in one direction, it produces some slack elsewhere? A viable industrial structure such as the one that has served Western societies for over two centuries would not have survived unless it could adapt to new circumstances and could internally generate incentives to adapt. This is not to say that there cannot be very bleak times, or that overcoming them is inevitable, but both are probable. By making unrelated assumptions about the economic variables that feed into market models, however, a mysterious black box replaces the structured model, and, human character being what it is in corporate planning departments, whenever the black box is opened up, the Four Horsemen of the Apocalypse will come charging out. The danger will be of over-pessimistic assumptions, bred of a myopic view of the economy, and when these are forced through the market and financial models, the managers will refuse to believe them. So there is no short-cut approach, no escape from properly structured models. We need to investigate their particular characteristics in more depth.

International v. national models

A two-group classification of macroeconomic models distinguishes between the purely national model and the integrated international model. One-country models typically—indeed, necessarily—treat influences from the rest of the world as input variables. The UK Treasury model, for instance, requires world prices, trade, production, and interest rates to be provided by assumption.[2] External influences are thus compressed into a handful of values (usually weighted to reflect their importance to the country concerned). These input values must again be internally consistent. It would be unacceptable to have fast growth in variables such as world industrial production and trade while assuming a very restrictive financial environment. In the multinational arena, however, achieving this consistency is not a simple matter, because of the size and complexity of the economics concerned. Indeed, this type of model is beginning to approach the sort of holism—trying to model the whole world—that is suspect.

Some consistency, however, can be achieved, at least in theory, with a series of linked models for a variety of countries. Normally the linkages would be through the trade sector, imports, and exports, including their prices, and through the financial sector, interest rates, capital flows, and exchange rates. Linked models avoid the problem of fallacy of composition. Wherever international input variables have to be fed into a national model, it is very tempting to tot up the growth rates being projected by other national forecasting agencies. However, if each country is achieving rapid growth via exports while restricting imports, it is logically impossible for the projected growth rates to be realized. Global exports must equal imports, and if they do not, then aggregate growth rates, obtained from national forecasts, will be wrong.

Another advantage that linked models share is that they deal much more consistently with changes in relative prices and trade balances. For instance, in 1979 the USA was following an exchange rate policy of 'benign neglect', which resulted in considerable pressure being exerted on the Deutschmark. While this was apparent at the time, what was less clear was how the Belgians and Dutch would be indirectly affected. National models for Germany in the right hands might have accurately captured the Deutschmark movement *vis-à-vis* the dollar, but it is less likely that Dutch and Belgian forecasters would have guessed the Deutschmark reaction and hence the way they would be affected.

Though consistency is desirable, linked models do have their drawbacks. It is not always the case that forecasts or scenarios for every country are needed. If a business has little trading contact with, say, Belgium there is no point in developing scenarios for that country, yet that part of the model cannot be totally unattended. Furthermore, as far as the user is concerned in this instance, solving for Belgium is a redundant cost. In order to keep costs within reasonable bounds the country models in a linked system are normally designed with fewer variables. This means they are individually less complex and hence more manageable. On the other hand, a limited output for each country can impose restraints on market linkages. If a market model has been designed for, say, plastic drain pipes and demand for these is heavily influenced by private housing expenditure, it would obviously be convenient if the macro-model generated this particular explanatory variable. However, such a series must be counted within the minutiae of economic data and would be

59

determined only by the more detailed national models, if at all. Linkage models would not normally produce such a series.

It is, therefore, for the multinational corporation that the linked models have the most obvious attractions, but the national business trading abroad should not ignore them. Thus, to approach once again the question of global consistency, if the US dollar slides *vis-à-vis* the Deutschmark it may have a certain set of implications for businesses based in Germany, but how would the Dutch guilder respond? The consequences might have arisen from the same economic disturbance, but their impact must be assessed from a variety of directions.

Typical output from a macro-model

Differences between national and linked models notwithstanding, it is possible to describe an archetypal model whose structure will not depart too much from specific variants. Great efforts have been made to harmonize national income accounts, but there is less congruity in other areas of macroeconomic statistics. Since model-builders have to use the materials that are available, the following outline is necessarily generalized. The level of generality is increased further by the inevitable theoretical differences that are incorporated in different models. Although economists have a penchant for engaging in recondite theoretical disputations—were not the economists on board the sinking *Titanic* arguing about the impact of icebergs on the shipping industry?—this need not produce great differences in structure.

For instance, some time ago there was great debate on the nature of the consumption function. One group argued that individual saving, and hence spending habits, were heavily influenced by the real (adjusted for inflation) value of their cash balances. Proponents claimed that, during periods of inflation, private cash balances would be eroded in real terms and people would, therefore, raise their saving rate and reduce consumption in order to restore the real worth of their savings; others dissented. The theoretical debate was about the nature of the consumption function, not about its existence. Therefore, the structure of the personal sector in two models could be virtually identical, though the specification of the consumption function would be different.

Similarity of model structure also arises from the fact that nearly all models seek to explain the expenditure definition of gross domestic product (GDP). GDP is the net value of output for a national economy in a given year. It can be measured in three ways, by totalling

- expenditure
- incomes
- production

60

These are three aspects of the same entity. Models, however, are invariably based on the expenditure data, which define GDP as:

$$
\begin{aligned}
\text{GDP} = \ &\text{private consumption} + \text{total investment} \\
&+ \text{government consumption} + \text{change in stocks} \\
&+ \text{exports} - \text{imports}
\end{aligned}
$$

To derive a volume measure of these expenditures they are expressed at constant prices, that is, at the price level prevailing in a base year. Many models will also have equations forecasting the movement in the price deflators so that volume figures can be multiplied by price to give a value series. Some models seek to derive both the income and production components of GDP, but these are normally driven by the expenditure variables.

Most models have at least six sectors with greater or lesser sophistication:

- personal
- company
- government
- trade
- prices and wages
- financial

A brief description of these six sectors follows, to indicate their relevance and importance.

Personal sector
The personal sector estimates total wages and salaries from average earnings derived in the prices and wages sector and from employment that is normally a function of the level of activity. To this is added government transfers, estimated in a government sector, and other incomes (rent, interest, dividends, and self-employment income). Tax payments are then deducted from total personal income to produce total disposable income. The latter is deflated by a suitable price index to determine real disposable income, which is an important input into the consumption function.

Company sector
The company sector seeks to explain private investment, inventory changes and employment. Investment functions vary considerably in their specification by different analysts. In the UK this is as much a result of a desperate search for something that will work tolerably well as it is of theoretical differences. Normally, a final sales term will appear to produce the familiar multiplier–accelerator concept, but other terms may be present also, such as

61

the cost of capital and corporate cash flow.[3] The equations for change in inventory are normally designed to capture the two types of inventory adjustment, planned and unintentional. This is one of the most volatile areas of the economy and perhaps the hardest to predict.

Government sector

The government sector deals with revenue-raising and expenditure (the latter in both volume and value terms) and the important fiscal deficit or surplus. Two major influences need to be caught: one is how the economic environment impinges on the fiscal deficit; and the other is how government policy is shaped to cope with its responsibilities of economic management. Variations in levels of economic activity can affect the fiscal deficit quite sharply; for instance, during a recession with falling demand and rising unemployment, tax revenues will fall (i.e., reduced sales, lower sales tax take, more unemployment, fewer taxpayers) and expenditure will rise (transfer payments to unemployed and their dependents). This systematic response is normally determined automatically within the tax and expenditure equations.

Policy changes, on the other hand, are best dealt with exogenously. Since governments are rarely sure of their policy moves from one day to the next, it seems a little unfair to ask a model to make a prediction. Many scenarios are likely to revolve around government action and reaction; therefore, there are substantial advantages in having a detailed government sector. For instance, a simple government sector might only have one variable, labelled 'indirect taxes', covering a wide range of tax bases and rates. If the scenario-planner wants to simulate petrol tax being raised, some thorny problems emerge. First, he cannot operate directly on a variable labelled petrol tax rate—there is none; second, he will not know from the model the tax base; and third, the model will not automatically estimate the effect on the retail price index. As a result, the user must make guesses in all these areas, until he can derive an approximate movement that needs to be made to those variables that are available. Obviously, the more levers to pull, the less that has to be guessed outside the model. The UK Treasury model, which was designed with these considerations very much in mind, permits the user to simulate a reasonably detailed policy stance, relatively simply.

Although it is invariably better to deal with policy changes via exogenous changes, a special situation arises with linked models. Suppose a scenario-planner wishes to raise the price of oil to reproduce yet another oil crisis. Besides raising the oil price in the model (assuming it is an integral feature), assumptions must be made about government responses world-wide. The scenario-planner may be interested in, or indeed have expertise in, only a handful of countries, yet half the model cannot be left without some form of government reaction. For example, the countries with which the model user is

62

concerned may, in the hands of the user, squeeze their economies in an attempt to reduce demand (which will limit all imports and dampen inflation). If governments in the other countries do not have their policies amended they will bear a great deal of the strain of readjustment. This may not have the makings of a realistic scenario. So what is there to do?

A second-best answer is to endogenize the government policy response. The best answer, of course, is to make specific assumptions about the response and deal with it exogenously in the model. The first alternative, nevertheless, can save both time and money and will amount to a more realistic set of adjustments than uninformed guesses or sheer neglect. Economic Models Ltd, for example, in its Diadem models has endogenized the policy element by devising a variable termed the 'constant employment financial deficit'. This adjusts past deficits for the variation in levels of demand and hence employment and, by removing those influences, reveals a series that expresses the fiscal policy stance of the government far more clearly.[4] This series is then regressed against selected indicators of economic performance, such as the balance of payments, inflation, and unemployment, for which governments have traditionally taken political responsibility. The quality of this relationship varies between countries, being quite good for the USA, where the concept is in fact all too familiar to policy-makers, and quite poor in the UK, where on the whole it has been ignored. With this sort of equation in the model, changes in economic conditions will generate a government response on the basis of past experience.

Trade sector
The trade sector determines both volumes and values of exports and imports. Trade in goods and services is invariably forecast since it is essential for the completion of the expenditure framework and is an important element in the balance of payments estimate. Exports tend to be a function of the level of foreign demand and relative prices or costs. The latter term will include the exchange rate. Imports, on the other hand, depend characteristically on domestic demand as well as on relative prices and costs. From the foregoing, not enough information is available to determine the balance of payments. Net transfer payments abroad need to be added, which include such items as government payments and receipts, net interest and dividends, and net capital investment.

In a linked model this sector is normally very large, because of the bilateral trade flows and price relationships. An equation is needed to deal with every trade partner of each country. However, unless the model is to become impossibly large, it has to be completed by aggregating countries into trading blocs. These might include OPEC countries, lesser developed countries (LDC), the small OECD countries, the Comecon nations, or quite simply the rest of the world. Whichever way the rest of the world outside the individual countries in the model are grouped, they need to make economic sense. If a grouping is seen as having distinguishing characteristics that affect its trading performance, then it will merit separate treatment.

Prices and wages sector
The prices and wages sector is a critical area of the model. It consists not only of domestic prices, but international prices and their interaction. Oil prices, international commodity prices, and the price of exports necessarily impinge on domestic prices. Wages depend on domestic prices and these in turn depend on wages. The simultaneous nature of prices and wages presents severe estimation problems; ordinary least squares is not normally adequate, and other techniques, such as two-stage least squares, have to be used. Furthermore, the history of direct government intervention in the price–wage system further complicates the interpretation of any estimated equation. The difference between the growth in prices and wages has a major influence on real incomes in the personal sector and hence on consumption. The entire trade balance via relative prices is equally affected, as is the company sector by virtue of the impact on cash flow and cost of capital. However, to emphasize the nature of simultaneity in any model, the influence of economic activity on prices and wages needs to be considered.

In the late 1950s, evidence was presented of an apparently very stable relationship between the change in money wage rates and the rate of unemployment.[5] The higher the rate of unemployment, the lower the rate of wage increases. Besides the obvious policy implications, this work indicated a volume feedback effect on price. Subsequently the relationship has appeared far from stable, and despite being amended, further analysis suggests that the unemployment effect is, at best, weak. However, periods of depressed demand have been known to set off price-cutting by businesses, and this too would represent a feedback. Another critical feature of the prices and wages sector is the way it interacts with foreign prices. Competitors exporting to Britain, for instance, finding that they have a cost advantage, have a choice. Do they undercut and go for greater market share, or do they aim for a particular market share and enjoy the corresponding profits? Much the same considerations apply to British exporters. The same problem of how much is absorbed in margin or transmitted in, say, price reductions arises with an appreciating currency. Import prices might come down or importers can enjoy improved margins. A well designed prices and wages sector must seek to capture these effects since they have an important bearing on domestic inflation and an even larger influence on the balance of payments.

Financial sector
The financial sector estimates such variables as money supply, interest rates, and the exchange rate. In recent years a great deal of effort has been put into

this sector by nearly all model designers in response to the debate over the rôle of money in capitalist economies. Policy prescriptions labelled 'monetarist' have advocated controlling the rate of growth in the money supply in order to suppress inflationary pressures; others labelled 'Keynesians' doubt the relationships between money supply and prices. The labels hide a multiplicity of views, but there is little doubt, whatever the merits of the arguments, that the intellectual body of economic opinion has shifted towards greater concern with monetary aggregates. As a result, the scope and significance of the financial sector has grown in most models. The UK Treasury model is a case in point—it now has a very extensive financial sector, though this does not make it a 'monetary' model, where nominal income and prices are determined, *inter alia*, by the money supply.[6] Examples of 'monetary' models are rare, but the St Louis model is in this category.[7]

The determination of the exchange rate, whether it is against the dollar, the pound, or in terms of the Smithsonian parity, is not always seen as a monetary variable. This is curious, since the exchange rate is the price of domestic money in terms of foreign money. It stems from the insistence on seeing the demand and supply of money on the foreign exchanges being nearly completely determined by the balance of payments on current account. In a world of widely fluctuating OPEC cash balances and floating exchange rates, autonomous capital flows are now more likely to dominate the demand–supply balance, and hence the exchange rate. Unfortunately, the success in forecasting these highly volatile variables has, so far, been unimpressive.

Simulating on a macro-model

How can these macro-models be used in practice? Virtually all time-sharing computer agencies with macroeconomic models will have available their own current forecast for the constituent countries. The user can simulate from this base—he may, for example, want to raise the average earnings assumption—by making adjustments to the residuals on the endogenous variables, or changing directly the values of the input terms. The simultaneity of the model will result in such a change rippling through the entire equation in a consistent fashion.

In fact, the user is obliged to simulate from the agency's current forecast base, because, on entering the model, he will inherit not an empty hulk, but one already crammed full of input values and residual adjustments. If he does not change either of these, the model will only produce the agency forecast. An alternative forecast, or scenario, requires a combination of input and residual changes. Altering input values is conceptually straightforward. If the model has exogenous oil prices running at a particular level over the forecast period, the user can simply input the series and make adjustments where necessary

65

before re-running the model. Making residual changes in the output variables is not so clear-cut.

It is worth briefly recalling the significance of residuals. This is an important point. In Chapter 4, market models were described as having equations with output and input terms. The output terms are determined by the model over the forecast period, while the input terms are provided by the user prior to running the model. The latter are, of course, his own assumptions. Appendix 4 describes how, in the estimation of regression equations, systematic influences are isolated, leaving a residual element that is random. In exactly the same way as for market models, the equations determining the output terms in the macro-models will estimate only the systematic component. Theoretically the random terms, the residuals, should tend to zero and ideally be very small. In practice this is not always the case. Either equation mis-specification or subsequent structural change in the real world will produce a residual that may appear neither random nor small. This is why it is essential, both in macroeconomic and market models, to keep a historical record of the developments in the residuals.

The residuals on the equations determining the output terms, therefore, have a life of their own. Setting all residuals to zero over the forecast period will invariably produce a nonsense. A view must be taken about their future course over the forecast as well as providing input values. Data on a computer is stored in files, so when the user gains access to the model he immediately inherits computer files containing residual adjustments and input values. If no other changes were made and the model were simply run, these files would be drawn upon and the current forecast would be reproduced. On the other hand, if the user added a further amount, for example to the average earnings residual term, this would temporarily create a new value for this residual while all the others, including the input values, remained unchanged. The owner of the model is, therefore, providing a service in supplying these residuals, since he is in one sense saving the user the effort of deciding how the residuals should be moving. Furthermore, he is offering his expertise as forecaster in providing judgements on the future course of the economy concerned. In a linked international model, the scenario-planner may have no 'feel' for those economies outside his immediate concern and may find it convenient to have the benefit of expert judgement.

Changing agency forecasts

What are the points to watch in actually making changes to the forecasts of these agencies? Suppose the forecast sees a situation of rising inflation and decides to build in a government response in the form of an incomes policy, by reducing the residual on average earnings. It might do this by operating on the average earnings residual. A client might agree with the prognosis, but disagree with the likely remedy. He may wish to simulate the government's adopting a much tighter fiscal and monetary stance. The client must now remove the adjustment to the earnings variable and then simulate his own policy reaction. The problem is, how much does he add back to the earnings residual?

If the projections had been calculated on the basis of a policy of 'smooth residuals', then he could deduce the adjustment.[8] Thus, if the forecasters had decided either to let the residuals follow their long-term trend, or to run them off at the last known actual value, it would be a simple matter in the earlier example to see where, and to what extent, there is a discontinuity in the average earnings variable. Of course, the user would need access to the historical residuals and forecasting agencies are not always so keen to make them available: since knowledge of the residuals gives a profound insight into the quality of the equations, it highlights its imperfections. The fact is that no model will be perfect in every respect. Agencies naturally fear that customers will not appreciate this and so are slow to release data on residuals.

If, on the other hand, the forecasters had decided to adopt a different approach to residuals and to prink and preen the model so that the forecast contained a substantial element of judgement, the adjustment would be very difficult to deduce indeed. The agency would have to either provide very good documentation or direct support from the individual forecasters. It might have to provide both. Without such assistance it would be impossible to alter meaningfully the projections or even generate new scenarios.

There is one final area where the use of a time-sharing system may have problems. Human nature being what it is, there is very little chance of a model's being built and then left forever in its pristine condition. Some equations, which are not totally acceptable but were used because they were the best available at the time, are likely to be revised. Sometimes the revisions can be extensive and change the entire sectoral structure. While it is necessary for users to be notified of such changes—good documentation is essential— with each respecification the user will lose his 'feel' for the model. For in the normal way, with practice and experience, a user will be able to develop an intuitive sense of how the model will respond to a change in a residual, and this is very valuable. The greater the feel for the model, the more cost effectively it can be used. Changes to the model that improve its technical efficiency, can, therefore, be a mixed blessing, since they erode user experience.

Residual changes

There are two broad manipulations that a user might want to make to the residuals in a macro-model. The first is where the forecaster wishes the integrity of the equations to be maintained and does not wish to impose discontinuities on the residuals. In this instance, he will want the residuals to reflect their past trend or perhaps remain at their last known level. In essence, the forecaster is trying to make the future residual pattern look somewhat similar to what has happened in the recent past. Some use autoregressive equations, where future values of the residual are a function of past values.

The second type of manipulation the user might wish to make involves introducing a discontinuity. He might feel that there are specific reasons accounting for a recent rise or fall in a residual, and that, since these factors have now been removed, the residuals should assume values appropriate to the prior conditions. In Fig. 5.1 two possibilities are shown: situation (a) reflects a one-off shock, perhaps a strike, where the residual has risen to a high level and there is every reason to believe that the situation will revert to its past pattern. Situation (b) represents a once-and-for-all shock, a step change,

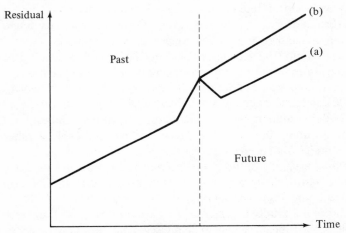

Figure 5.1 Types of discontinuities

where the residual moves to a new level and is not expected to revert at all. For instance, an excise tax may have been introduced which has shifted the retail price index to a new level.

If the equation whose residual is being manipulated is linear, then a once-and-for-all shock would be represented by the addition of a constant residual throughout the forecast period. Alternatively, if a one-off shock were being simulated on a linear equation, then an amount would be added in one time period, but not in the next. This simple manipulation can be complicated by certain forms of equations. Take, for example, a difference equation; this could be in logarithms or in natural values:

$$Y_t - Y_{t-1} = a + bX_t + E_t \qquad (5.1)$$

In the above equation the right-hand side of the equation is explaining the

68

difference in Y. If Y were in logs it would effectively be explaining the percentage change. But consider the implications of increasing the residual E in period t when the equation is rewritten thus:

$$Y_t = a + bX_t + E_t + Y_{t-1} \qquad (5.2)$$

Let t equal 1, so that an increase in E_t raises the value of Y in period one by the amount of the increase. In period two, the calculation of Y starts with the value it achieved in the previous period, which contained an additional residual adjustment. If the intention of the residual adjustment in period one were to produce a once-and-for-all upward shift, then no further residual changes would be needed in subsequent periods. On the other hand, if the intention were to generate a one-off shock, then it would be necessary to remove in period two the amount added in period one.

A final complication that arises from the structure of the equation, occurs when the model designer encounters autocorrelation (i.e., when future error term values are dependent on past values) and solves the problem by a transform (see Appendix 4). The equation form containing the autocorrelation may have been:

$$Y_t = a + bX_t + E_t \qquad (5.3)$$

which, when transformed to remove the autocorrelation, looks like

$$Y_t - (\rho)Y_{t-1} = a\,[1 - (\rho)] + b\,[X_t - (\rho)X_{t-1}] + E_t \qquad (5.4)$$

This equation is not unlike (5.1), inasmuch as the dependent variable, Y, appears as a difference on the left-hand side. In fact if rho (ρ) equalled 1, it would be a simple difference equation and the warning mentioned earlier would apply. If, on the other hand, ρ took a value close to 0, the equation would be indistinguishable from a normal linear equation and manipulation of its residual could be treated accordingly. However, if ρ takes a value between 0 and 1, say 0.5, then a residual added to Y in period one will be fully reflected in that period, half of it in the next period and half of that in the period following, and so on. In this instance, a quite complex set of adjustments needs to be made to reflect one-off or once-and-for-all shocks.

Additional operation options

So far, discussion on the manipulation of the model has centred on changing input values, or making residual changes on equations estimating output terms. However, with a little more sophisticated programming on the part of the model designers, it is possible to perform additional operations on the model. Most models allow the user to exogenize an endogenous term. Thus, for part of the forecast period, or all of it, the user can decide the value of any variable. This is particularly useful when simulating scenarios, because the

69

planner can be sure that the target value will be achieved precisely by the model at the first time of asking.

This is not always the case with changing residuals. An increase in a residual, in a simultaneous system, will, on the first iteration, raise the value of the output term to which it is applied. This, in turn, results in new values for the other equations in the simultaneous system, which feed back to the original equation. When the model has finally converged, the adjusted output value need not be the simple addition of the residual and the last solution value of the model. Therefore, if a user wishes to simulate the effect of average earnings tumbling very quickly in a recession and he has a notional rate in mind, he will achieve it exactly at the first go by exogenizing it, but might need more attempts if he were seeking to hit his target by residual manipulation.

Agencies offering models can help their clients with this problem by generating a cross-impact file. This computer file is produced by tweaking each variable one at a time by, say, 1 per cent via its residual and then noting the percentage change of all variables including the adjusted variable itself. This is very expensive but provides very useful information, not only about the sensitivity of the model to adjustments in the current time period, but about how the changes unwind over time.

Another useful facility, one that is on the UK Treasury model and revels in the name of a 'type II fix', allows the user to achieve an imposed value for a particular output variable by getting one of its determinants to adjust sufficiently. Thus, if the government were seen to be seeking to impose a particular growth path on the money supply, it would be possible to impose that on the model and then see what interest rates would be required to achieve it. It is substantially useful for scenario-builders since it readily permits policy simulations in the most effective manner.

The various devices mentioned so far—adjusting exogenous values, altering residuals and fixing endogenous values—can be combined to change the forecast inherited from the time-sharing agency. Chapter 8 gives an example of how an oil scenario was developed. However, it is apparent from the foregoing that macro-models do not have scenario buttons marked 'oil crisis', 'wages freeze', and so on, merely requiring to be pushed. The user himself must design and administer the initial scenario shock to the equation system and then trace through the numerical story that the model will, in consequence, relate.

The story may not be complete at first, or entirely consistent, because the changes made are still partial and do not adequately reflect all the implications of the initial shock. The user refines the impact to take care of the omissions and applies his own judgement to the results. Some equations will not produce the results anticipated, and the user must decide whether his own predispositions are correct, and the equation in these circumstances fails to take account of significant developments, or whether he has not allowed for certain

70

influences that the model considers important. The model does not run unconstrained, but is being challenged by, and itself challenges, the user. Man and machine converge to a solution that is finally acceptable to man.

Compatibility with market models

The final output of a macro-model will be a computer file containing numerous macroeconomic variables. Some of these will be the input values of the market models. There must, therefore, be a ready means of feeding the data to these models. It is desirable to have as much compatibility between them and the macroeconomic output. Normally this happens by force of circumstance, since the agency owning the models will have had to collect a large historical macro-data base on the various countries it plans to model. Furthermore, it needs a good statistical package to derive the equations. Both of these are required by the market modeller, since he will need macroeconomic data as his input terms as well as the tool of regression, etc. Thus, by model-building from the data base used by the agency to generate its macro-models, a high degree of compatibility is achieved and common definitions may be ensured. Both the variables' names and the units will be the same (e.g., thousands of pounds at 1975 prices).

Although compatibility is desirable, it is nevertheless dangerous to tailor market models solely to the immediate output of the macro-models. If, for theoretical reasons, there are good grounds for including a variable in the market models that is not generated from the macro-model, two alternatives are available. Either the values have to be provided by assumption, or an equation must be derived for the exogenous term from the variables forecast by the macro-models. In principle this could result in endless back-tracking, but in practice this is most unlikely to be unlimited. The model designer should, however, always be guided by the principles of sound theory.

In summary, therefore, the macro-models provide pictures of the environment that are both complete and consistent. They can cope with the simultaneity of the real world, while an individual is limited to thinking through one step at a time.

Notes

1. L. R. Klein and R. M. Young, *An Introduction to Econometric Forecasting and Forecasting Models*, Lexington Books, D. C. Heath & Co., Toronto, 1980.
2. *H.M. Treasury Macro-Economic Model Technical Manual 1979*, H.M. Treasury, London, 1979. It should be noted that the Treasury also has a World Economic Prospects (WEP) model, which provides many of the exogenous variables needed by the UK model.
3. R. C. O. Matthews, *The Trade Cycle*, Cambridge University Press, Cambridge, 1959, pp. 8–17.

4. A concept familiar to the USA, but not widely used in UK: see F. T. Blackaby (ed.), *British Economic Policy 1960–74*, Cambridge University Press, Cambridge, 1978, chs 3 and 4.
5. A. W. Phillips, 'The relationship between unemployment and the rate of change in money wage rates in the United Kingdom, 1861–1957', *Economica*, 25, 1, 283–99, 1958.
6. P. Spencer, C. Mowl, R. Lomax, and M. Denham, *A Financial Sector for the Treasury Model*, Government Economic Service Working Paper no. 17, H.M. Treasury, London, 1978.
7. K. M. Carlson, 'A monetarist model for economic stabilisation', *Federal Reserve Bank of St Louis Review*, April 1970, pp 7–23. Also, for an application to UK economy see K. G. P. Matthews and P. A. Ormerod, 'St Louis models of the UK economy', *National Institute Economic Review (NIER)*, no. 84, May 1978, pp 65–9.
8. Some forecasters occasionally make use of auto-regressive rules, where future values of the errors are some function of past errors: see P. Ormerod and M. J. C. Surrey, 'Formal and informal aspects of forecasting with econometric models', *NIER*, no 81, August 1977, pp. 67–71. D. R. Osborne and F. Teal, 'An assessment and comparison of two NIESR econometric model forecasts', *NIER*, no. 88, May 1979, pp. 50–62.

6.
The base-case scenario

The need for common assumptions

The space-station we described in Chapter 1 is at war—not the shooting sort, but a commercial conflict, fought with varying degrees of intensity with every other competitor in its market places. So long as the messages flashing between the commander-in-chief and his operating units are clear and logical, he gets good intelligence and can maintain control. It would require a very special sort of madness, therefore, given a well engineered space-ship and competent crew, to allow all the unit commanders to invent their own code for communicating their dispositions and tactics. It might be feasible to work such a system if they let on to HQ how to operate the code, though this does not seem a very efficient approach. But if the details of the code are not known, chaos reigns.

Our own experience in this context of a common code of economic assumptions has been mixed. When we first started planning on a structured basis, we handed down key assumptions. With massive external fluctuations occurring between this hand-out and the conclusion of business plans, it became clear that managers who were going to be committed to the performance of these plans were less than happy to adopt these assumptions. If there had been a marked deterioration in growth or a significant rise in inflation, such that there were major changes in the platform for launch into the business year and in the direction of the forces affecting the flight-path, they wanted to take these into account. So we tried going the route of 'use your own code, but tell us what it is'. We then expected to be able to 'normalize' their forecasts to our own base-case. This worked even less well. In many cases, the variables adopted were internally inconsistent; in others, no links were convincingly established between the guidelines and the forecasts of performance; and in the worst cases it was not apparent that any assumptions had been used at all!

The problem of actually getting managers to base their predictions on a specific scenario in any clear-cut way will, however, always be with us. It's a question of competence, understanding, and education. The problem of inconsistent (and, indeed, total absence of) assumptions, however, has to be solved at once. Any plan must be governed by the same story. A forecast of an economy tells that story in terms of events unfolding and a society responding to stimuli. It is not just a set of numbers, even though it is often represented as such.

So one business might envisage a general economic recession and losses, while another might see a boom and bumper profits. Sitting at the corporate centre, the profits of one appear to offset the losses of the other and the chief executive pulls on his cigar and pontificates to his peers on his brilliance in putting together a well-balanced group. If he doesn't know what assumptions each business used, or can't put a picture together on common guidelines, he is likely to get a surprise—though it could be a nice surprise, just as well as a nasty one.

The nature of the base-case

It seems, then, that there is no escaping the need, in a large multi-product corporation, to issue common economic guidelines—a base-case scenario. But what should be the nature of such a scenario? Should it provide a range of forecasts, or only a single-line set of key factors?

In a world of limitless managerial resource and time, it would be desirable to provide a number of different scenarios to each activity and permit its executives to think through the impact each would have on its performance. This would in fact bring two benefits. First, local business experience is being used to consider the effects each scenario would have on the individual trading climate and what the response would be under those circumstances. Second, it would be a good exercise in corporate crisis management. In projecting the corporation into an assumed situation, it may be discovered that the organization does not, in fact, have the skills or flexibility required. That would be a very salutary discovery, and might initiate early action in management development.

However, line management, making a desperate stand against the enemy of today is going to be dismissive of invitations to fight simultaneously on a number of imaginary fronts. So the tendency is to limit the exercise severely.

This does not mean, however, that the standard hand-down of a dozen or so key variables based on a single underlying view of events is the solution to this problem. At the time of writing, Shell Oil, for example, does not provide a central forecast as the basis for plans. Various scenarios are prepared, but, by the time these reach the business units, they have normally been condensed into ranges of key factors. This system is evidently both useful and practicable and marries together two sets of skills. The first set lies with the scenario-planners, who can analyse social, political, and economic trends. The second set lies with the activity management, who should be able to interpret the implications for their respective businesses and design suitable responses. For a company that is largely dependent on one product, and which, furthermore, has a high degree of vertical integration, this system seems highly appropriate. There may be a limited number of key variables that affect the business in a fundamental way—the price of oil is an obvious example. Oil being what it is, the rate of growth of the economy as measured by GDP might be an adequate surrogate for demand. Scenarios could then be grouped by growth rates and oil prices to produce archetypes which can then be issued to the business units.

Imagine, on the other hand, a conglomerate that produces, among other things, trucks and magazines. The economic parameters that guide the fortunes of each market are entirely different. For instance, econometric analysis suggests that real disposable income is a key variable in explaining the new registrations of trucks. Similar analysis for magazine advertising suggests that it is sensitive to aggregate corporate profits. It is not difficult to envisage a situation where, taking the two activities together, a rising real disposable income could be associated with either rising or falling profits. Circumstances will dictate which. This makes archetypal analysis much harder and perhaps impossible to apply. Once again, the emphasis is placed on presenting a consistent picture of the environment, so that each activity can take the elements that are important to it and project them on to its own business environment.

Comparing the forecasters

The big practical question for the planner at this point is: 'which particular forecast should I adopt? Which of the agencies has been nearest to the bulls-eye?' An idea of the risk being taken when plans are based on a single forecast can be gauged by looking at the various track records of forecasters. Regrettably, this is not a very reassuring exercise, and is a major argument for scenario planning.

Measuring the accuracy of forecasting agencies is not, in fact, as simple as it appears. First, the objective needs to be specified. Is the intention to find the best overall forecaster, or only how well a given variable is forecast by a particular agency? In the latter instance, a business may be peculiarly dependent upon a specific variable that is predicted by only one forecaster. In this event the business has no choice; nonetheless, it is at least worth while knowing how well or badly the agency is faring. If, on the other hand, a business is seeking the best overall forecaster, then the matter becomes more complex.

It is necessary to compare like with like. This boils down to comparing the same variables over the same time period. Unfortunately, different models have different specifications, so the output is not identical in all respects. Furthermore, the operations of present forecasting agencies have spanned different periods, during which they have changed their model output either by introducing new variables or dropping old ones. The practical attempt to measure forecasting accuracy for the same set of variables over a common time-span suffers, therefore, from remarkably severe restrictions.

In the United Kingdom, the National Institute of Economic and Social Research (NIESR), the London Business School (LBS), the Treasury, and the Henley centre have been forecasting for many years. More recently, however, a spate of new agencies has come forward, particularly among the stock-broking community. From the handful of variables common to all over a meaningful period, how is overall performance to be assessed? Are all variables to be given equal importance, or are some more important than others? In practice, each user will want to weight the variables according to his own schedule of preferences, so it is impossible to make any unequivocal claim that X has the best forecasting record. Furthermore, past achievements do not necessarily promise future successes.

The techniques for comparison

In undertaking the analysis, a comparison must be made for each variable, between predicted and actual. Forgetting for the moment the habit of government statistical offices to rewrite economic history well into the recesses of time, the best form of comparison is between rates of change rather than absolute levels. Most economic data indicate an upward movement over the years, either under the impact of inflation or owing to economic growth. To prevent trend influences swamping the comparison, attention is focussed on the rate of change.

$$A_t = 100 \ (a_t - a_{t-1})/a_{t-1} \qquad \text{actual rates of change} \qquad (6.1)$$

$$P_t = 100 \ (p_t - a_{t-1})/a_{t-1} \qquad \text{predicted rates of change} \qquad (6.2)$$

where a denotes the actual level of the variable concerned, p the predicted level, A the period rate of change in a, and P the rate of change in p relative to the last known actual. Figure 6.1 represents the type of errors that can be made in forecasting. Each dot $(C_1 - C_6)$ represents a plot for a P_t and its corresponding A_t. A perfect forecast, where $P_t = A_t$, would produce a 45° line passing through the origin (see broken line). Quadrant 1 of the graph (Q1) represents the situation where P_t is less than A_t and furthermore is negative when the actual change is positive. Thus, besides underestimating, the prediction is either suggesting a turning-point when one has not occurred, or has failed to capture an actual turning-point. Much the same is shown by quadrant 3 (Q3), except that the prediction is an overestimate. Quadrant 2 (Q2) illustrates the situation where the prediction is right in terms of direction, i.e., positive rate of growth but where C_1 represents underestimation, C_2 shows overestimation. Quadrant 4 (Q4) is similar in character, except that the rate of change is negative.

By studying the term $P_t - A_t$, deviations from the 45° line may be analysed. The technique measures the mean error (ME):

$$ME = \frac{\sum (P_t - A_t)}{N} \qquad (6.3)$$

(where N is the number of observations). The sign of the mean error reveals

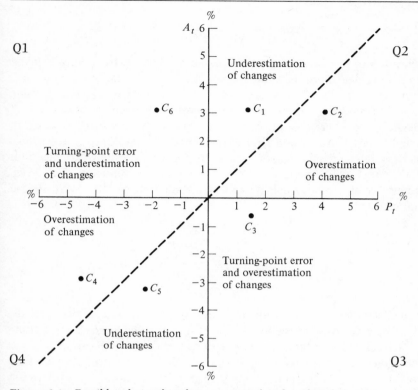

Figure 6.1 Possible relationships between actual and predicted change

whether, on average over the period, the tendency has been to over- or underestimate. However, from this measure, it cannot be ascertained whether the result was achieved from many small positive deviations being offset by a massive single negative. Furthermore, the offsetting characteristics tend to understate the error. This can be resolved, however, by using the average absolute error (*AAE*):

$$AAE = \frac{\sum | P_t - A_t |}{N}.$$ (6.4)

This measure ignores the sign, treating all deviations as positive, and so is an improvement as a measure of overall error. However, it treats all errors equally. In principle, there could be produced identical average absolute errors from two series, one of which had modest consistent errors and another which had erratic, large, and small errors. It is desirable to give the larger errors extra weight, since grossly misleading forecasts are those that should be penalized. This is achieved with the root mean square error (*RMSE*):

77

$$RMSE = \sqrt{\left(\frac{\sum (P_t - A_t)^2}{N}\right)}. \qquad (6.5)$$

By squaring the deviations and then summing them, extra weight is being given to large deviations. Like the average absolute error, there is no tendency of errors to cancel in this measure, but it is not possible, either, to determine whether the tendency was to over- or underestimate over the period.

There is one other attribute of prediction that ought to be incorporated into a measure of accuracy, and that is the inherent volatility of the variable concerned. It is somewhat less impressive to forecast accurately variables with smooth paths than those with violent changes of direction. The Theil inequality coefficient (U) achieves this by standardizing the $RMSE$ by the actual variability.

$$U = \frac{\sqrt{\frac{1}{N} \sum (P_t - A_t)^2}}{\sqrt{\frac{1}{N} \sum A_t^2}}. \qquad (6.6)$$

The coefficient has several useful properties. When $P = A$ for all time periods, $U = 0$; thus the smaller the value of U, the better the forecast. Something approaching an upper limit can be formulated when the implication of $P = 0$ is considered. If there were a consistent 'no change' prediction for all time periods, then $U = 1$. Therefore, if $U > 1$, it means that a more accurate forecast would have been achieved by assuming no change at all in the variable. The Theil coefficient also permits tests against simplistic alternative models. For instance, it might be said that $P_t = A_{t-1}$, i.e., the predicted rate of change will be the same as the one last experienced. This assumption will produce a U value that can be used as a benchmark for assesseing the predictions of forecasting agencies. The above 'naïve model' probably represents what most people tend to assume in the absence of the plethora of macroeconomic model forecasts. The comparison might be seen as illustrating how well people would fare without forecasting agencies.

Few forecasting agencies actually publish their track record in terms of the statistics described above. NIESR, to their credit, do so on a regular basis.[1] Studies conducted on the track record of UK forecasting prior to the first oil crisis show that U values were, on the whole, below unity and lower than the values of the naive models.[2] During, and for some time after, the oil crisis forecasts deteriorated somewhat, since the change in prices had brought about structural changes in many economies.[3] Our own analysis is shown in Table 6.1 for various UK agencies with a long track record over a fairly narrow range of variables. The comparisons are based on one-year predictions issued around August–September, a period relatively free of budgets and policy changes.

Table 6.1 Analysis of selected forecasting agencies' projections

Agency	A	P	ME	AAE	$RMSE$	U_0	U_1	U_2	Span
NIESR									
Con. spend.	1.638	1.548	−0.09	1.171	1.484	0.524	0.809	1.132	1968–77
GDP	1.828	2.609	0.781	2.231	2.631	0.842	1.257	2.150	1968–77
Con. prices	10.928	8.736	−2.192	3.432	4.161	0.336	0.352	0.490	1968–77
LBS									
Con. spend.	1.638	1.373	−0.265	0.662	0.787	0.278	0.809	1.132	1968–77
GDP	1.828	2.695	0.867	1.680	1.933	0.619	1.257	2.150	1968–77
Henley									
Con. spend.	1.654	3.146	1.492	1.877	2.700	0.889	0.819	1.159	1970–77
GDP	1.630	3.077	1.447	2.793	3.179	0.991	1.353	2.326	1970–77
Con. prices	12.357	7.625	−4.732	4.997	6.043	0.445	0.337	0.464	1970–77

Key
A = mean of actual rate of change
P = mean of predicted rate of change
ME = mean error
AAE = average absolute error
$RMSE$ = root mean square error
U_0 = Theil inequality coefficient for forecast
U_1 = Theil inequality coefficient for naive model $P_t = A_{t-1}$
U_2 = Theil inequality coefficient for naive model $P_t = A_{t-1} + (A_{t-1} - A_{t-2})$
Con. spend. = consumer spending
GDP = gross domestic product

Adopting a specific base-case

The first principle in adopting a base-case is that it should be as free of controversial hunches or guesses about the future as may be. This forecast will provide the base from which all other scenarios are simulated. If it were to contain strong, quirkish assumptions about the distant future that would be logically incompatible with the majority of alternative scenarios contemplated, these assumptions would have to be eliminated before proceeding with the exercise. This represents an unnecessary and expensive complication. Thus, the simulation base should contain the best middle-of-the-road prediction of the future; adventure should be saved for the alternative scenarios.

The most cost-effective source of an uncontentious base-case scenario is likely to be from a forecasting agency such as was described in Chapter 5. All necessary data should be available for running the market models to establish activity forecasts on a consistent basis. But there may be good reasons for rejecting, in some part, the totality of the agency's forecast. In particular, in a multinational organization, a local headquarters might reasonably take an alternative view about its own economy.

The same kind of difficulty can recur later in the scenario-generating process. Suppose that an acceptable base forecast has been derived from the macro-models, at the beginning of the planning round (say, August). The activities will draw up their plans appropriately. By the time they have reported back in December, however, it is quite conceivable that the macro-model agency will have put up a new forecast. Now, unless the user has taken precautions to save his residual adjustments and input values in his own computer files, he will have lost his base-case. This may or may not be a problem, depending on whether he wishes to simulate scenarios from his base-case or from the new forecast. Perhaps of more importance is that, in the intervening period, economic developments may have been sufficient to change the *character* of the agency forecast. These new developments would have to be incorporated in the user's own base-case.

So the problem boils down to this: is the new forecast still acceptable, both in itself and for providing an adequate base for future scenarios? If it is not acceptable, the user must make his own new forecast. He could do this from his own saved base-case, or he could adjust the current agency forecast. Where he is using a linked model, however, it normally remains advantageous to use the new agency forecast; it will have updated developments in sectors or territories where he has little interest, or perhaps no detailed knowledge; as we indicated earlier, he can't ignore these, whatever his level of concern or ignorance. Even with single country models it is probably worth taking the new forecast, as it is likely to reflect, if not all, at least many of the new developments to the user's satisfaction.

There are two occasions when the user has to make a choice between adopting the agency forecast and making extensive changes to it. The first is when drawing up the base-case for the plans. The second is when a new base, incorporating all intervening developments, has to be designed. Of course, the user may be lucky. He might find the agency forecasts on both occasions fully satisfactory. It is rare, however, that he will get away without some manipulation.

In subsequent chapters we provide a worked example of a scenario from beginning to end. We created a mythical corporation, Conglom Ltd, and developed a base economic case for this purpose. To avoid excessive detail, while preserving the illustrative features of the exercise, the description is limited to the UK. The UK base-case, in fact, followed one produced by an agency towards the end of 1979. Since this was essentially short-term, it was necessary to fix the macro-model to reproduce the early year's results and then extend them into later years upon consistent assumptions.

In Table 6.2 the parameters that are a very small subset of the available projections, give a picture of the base case adopted. This Base-Case (we

Table 6.2

	1980	1981	1982	1983	1984	1985
GDP (%)	−0.5	1.9	4.0	5.3	4.3	2.7
GDP deflator	12.2	9.5	8.1	7.3	9.0	10.2
$/£	2.20	2.15	2.06	2.06	2.06	2.06

distinguish it with capitals) foresaw a mild recession, with inflation coming down mildly, against a background of a government's controlling its borrowing and money supply. This meant it would be able to pass on hefty tax cuts from burgeoning North Sea oil revenues. Combined with strong productivity improvement, there was to be a sustained boom, imports being sucked in but inflation not accelerating wildly. The Base-Case was prepared in the early days of monetarist euphoria.

The output from the macro-models feeds into the market models to generate 'shadow' values for the Base-Case. These are used to quantify the subsequent scenario changes relative to the base as described in Chapter 2. By the time the business plans have been prepared by the activities (on the Base-Case), events have moved on, and it is apparent that the outcomes of 1980 and 1981 are going to be very different. Adjustments have to be made to the Base-Case projections in order to initiate scenarios from a more accurate simulation base. Although the amendments provide a more credible point for simulations, all changes fed into the financial model are still measured relative to the Base-Case. The new simulation base is shown in Table 6.3. The squeeze on the economy is projected to produce a very powerful decline in economic activity. This brings down inflation and interest rates, generating a powerful recovery that is boosted further by tax cuts, funded by North Sea Oil revenue growth. Unemployment reaches very high levels.

At the time of adoption these projections were very much in line with what the majority of forecasters were saying. In the real world, however, it is certain that this set would not occur as specified. Unease about the predictive quality could be dispelled only by the use of scenarios that explored the major areas of uncertainty and enabled consideration of how robust the plans might be to

Table 6.3

	1980	1981	1982	1983	1984	1985
GDP (%)	−3.4	−1·4	4.2	6.7	6.1	2.1
GDP deflator	16.6	13.3	8.0	4.9	6.3	9.3
$/£	2.33	2.29	2.29	2.31	2.32	2.32

changes. So, it is to an examination of such alternative scenario that we turn in Chapter 8.

Notes

1. D. R. Osborn, 'National Institute gross output forecasts: a comparison with US performance', *NIER*, no. 88, May 1979; A. J. H. Dean, 'Errors in National Institute forecast of personal incomes, inflation and employment, 1965–75', *NIER*, no. 78, November 1976.
2. J. C. K. Ash and D. J. Smyth, *Forecasting the United Kingdom Economy*, Saxon House, Farnborough, Hants, 1973.
3. Osborn, op. cit., p. 49.

7.
Manipulating the data base

A 'duplicate' corporation

The blueprint of our system has now been laid out and studied and we are in a position to start some limited manoeuvres—to see how the manipulation of the data base will provide insights into the business. For this purpose we have to play at cosmic tycoons, and create our own mythical corporation: Conglom Ltd. While, in theory, we could develop a very wide spectrum of activities for this corporation and organize it into many divisions and subdivisions, such as would satisify even the most megalomaniacal chief executive officer, we shall limit ourselves to a modest four activities, and we shall not involve ourselves in any subsidiary consolidation.

A mock set of plan schedules is set out in Appendix 3, including:

	Schedule
• Summary	1
• Cash flow	2
• Balance sheet	3
• Profit and loss	4
• Activities	5–8

These are derived from real-life cases, though all have been disguised to some extent and they are from different corporations. All but one (Consumer Manufacturers) are deemed to operate in the UK; the exception is Dutch-based. The base-case economic assumptions are those discussed in Chapter 6. The history takes in 1975–78; 1979 is the current year for these purposes; and the plan years are 1980–82. The projections by the Activities are deliberately limited to three years as this must be the maximum time over which it is worth getting detailed forecasts. Beyond this, the impact of change may be examined by projecting the numbers. This has the effect of magnifying the impact and making clearer the implications of alternative courses of action.

To give a flavour of how all this information may be used in practice, the Conglom figures are treated in the form of a much simplified business plan analysis. The first task is a review of the overall trends to see whether the projections represent a credible and sufficient plan on the basis of the common environmental assumptions. This gives a feel for the variables that should be investigated for alternative values and tests the operational validity. We are avoiding getting into questions such as objectives and strategic guidelines: for this purpose we assume that the corporation is attempting to optimize growth at a minimum ROTC of 22 per cent in the long term. The individual activity strategies will emerge during the course of the discussion.

Sales, price and volume

Sales show some cyclicality in the period 1975–79, but the figures are given in current £. Weighting the underlying volume indices of the constituent activities to give a corporate volume index, the historical trends can be extracted and the forecasts judged (see Fig. 7.1). The graph shows in 1976 an

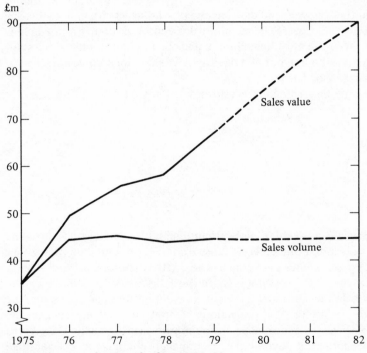

Figure 7.1   Total external sales, 1975–82

upward surge in volume in line with the surge in economic activity in that year, plus a 10 per cent price increase (somewhat lower than inflation, since we are using mainly the UK as our market place). This occurs during the recovery from recession. Volume, represented by deflated sales, flattens off after 1976 as the recovery reaches a plateau. The projections likewise show no increase. While the sales value appears to have the usual optimistic 'lift-off' in the plan period, in fact prices are forecast to rise by less than 10 per cent year upon year, which is more or less in line with Base Case inflation. So, apart from

84

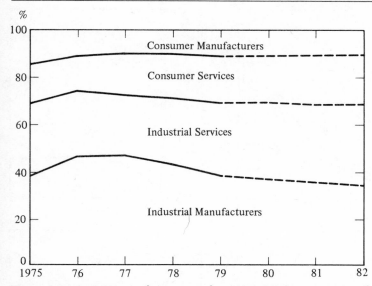

Figure 7.2 Activity contributions to sales, 1975–82. Consumer Manufacturers given in constant D.fl./£ at 1979 level

1976, a very modest performance is proposed, and for the future, a restrained forecast which indicates no real growth ambitions.

The underlying mix, however, indicates a much less comfortable situation. The relative importance of the activities by sales is shown in Fig. 7.2. Consumer Manufacturers, a Dutch company, is converted to sterling, with consequent exchange distortions, but as a measure of importance to Conglom, the figures are valid.

Consulting the Activity Schedules shown in Appendix 3, Schedules 5–8 and Fig. 7.3, it is seen that the first activity (Schedule 5), which we call Industrial Services Ltd, shows a steadily rising volume after a dip in 1977, but in the first plan year prices are also forecast to rise by 15 per cent. Can volume be sustained with such a major rise, or would it reduce and recover? Note that 1980 in the Base Case was the inflationary year allied to 0.6 per cent GDP recession. It is clear from 1977 experience that the direction is not always upwards. The volume increases proposed in the plan years are, however, lower than previously, so the policy looks very much like a gentle milking of the market.

The second activity, Consumer Services Ltd (Schedule 6), seems more convincing. When prices rose 14 per cent in 1979, volume also rose 5 per cent. The likelihood of being able to achieve in the first plan year a price increase of 16 per cent with a volume drop of 2 per cent is reasonably high and is in line with the economy, particularly in that average earnings are 21 per cent up in 1980, fuelling consumer expenditure. Again, a milking strategy is evident.

85

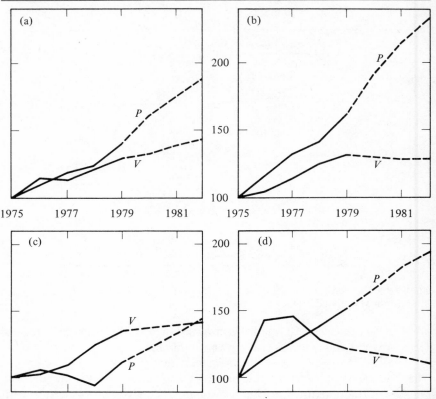

Figure 7.3 Sales indices, 1975–82: *P*, price; *V*, volume; index: 1975 = 100. (a) Industrial Services; (b) Consumer Services; (c) Consumer Manufacturers; (d) Industrial Manufacturers

Next comes Consumer Manufacturers BV (Schedule 7). A different approach is working through here. The concentration has been on volume, not price. At least temporarily, the price level has gone down in 1978 as the activity goes for market share. Just to jump ahead for a moment and link up the other factors, new investment being put in to sustain this market approach is being injected in 1977 and 1978 and losses are, hopefully, to be turned to profit—though even by the end of the plan period the ROTC is an unexiting 14.5 per cent. Nevertheless, it is a classic case of a turn-round by a strategy of seeking dominance in a growing market. The forecast numbers, however, indicate that the strategy is changing: prices are now being pushed ahead, while volumes remain more or less static.

Finally, there is Industrial Manufacturers Ltd (Schedule 8). The big leap in volume in 1976 was not sustained for more than a year. A rather lack-lustre management stance seems to be adopted: an unimaginative pricing policy traces a virtually straight line up the graph while another in the opposite direction indicates a continuing fall in volume. A more positive approach to the market could maintain a viable position. Should this be attempted, or should management continue to harvest the business as fast as at present? In fact, part of the decline comes from a reduction in the total market size, and with such a poor ROTC (4 per cent planning to rise to 12 per cent, as indicated in Schedule 8) it might be a case for disposal or a faster shrinking of the activity. For the time being, however, the plan figures seem at least credible. By the end of the period, it ceases to be the dominant activity in sales terms, though it is still significant.

Costs

The cost structure of Conglom has moved somewhat over the past four years. A big change occurred in 1976 when, in addition to some inflationary pressures and an increase in volume on the upside of the cycle, Industrial Manufacturers moved to new premises, adding a new element of cost. Since then, there has been a reversion to 1975 proportions.

Leaving aside depreciation, raw materials constitute the largest item— over one-third of the total—while almost another third are attributable to employment (see Fig. 7.4). Conglom is fortunate that only a relatively small part of the total relates to energy. It is, therefore, less directly susceptible to

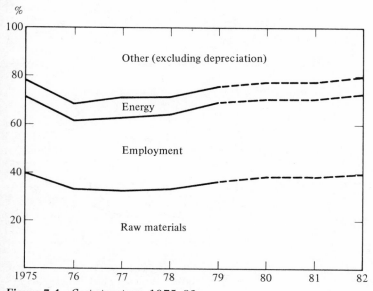

Figure 7.4 Cost structure, 1975–82

Middle-East crises than many, but we shall consider later how badly oil price inflation may affect demand for its products.

Looking at these items by activity, it is Industrial Manufacturers that, in 1978, reined in the accelerating pace of its raw materials costs, as a necessary corollary to its volume run-down (Fig. 7.5). On the other hand, Industrial Services, which is looking to increase volume in the future, shows a rise in the rate at which its raw material prices are increasing. On employment costs, the

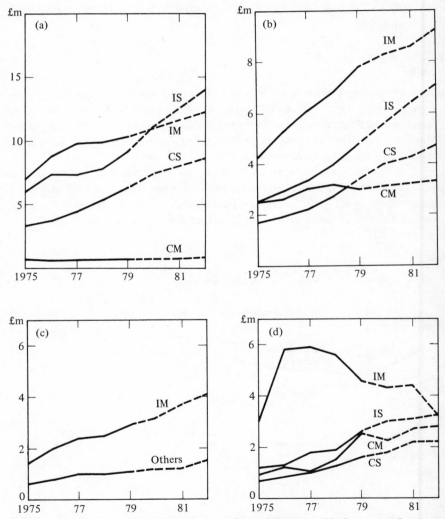

Figure 7.5 Cost analysis, 1975–82: IS, Industrial Services; CS, Consumer Services; CM, Consumer Manufacturers; IM, Industrial Manufacturers. (a) Raw materials costs; (b) Employment costs; (c) Energy costs; (d) Other costs

history is affected by Consumer Manufacturers closing a factory and concentrating manufacture in another, introducing at the same time a significant degree of automation. So in 1979 employment costs fall in this activity, though not by as much as planned. Note that severance payments are dealt with as 'extraordinary' costs. For the remainder, Industrial Manufacturers indicates a future improvement in trend—by 12 per cent, compared with 17 per cent in the past; this may result to a degree from the expected run-down in volume, but no costs of severance have been allowed for to indicate a commensurate run-down in the labour force.

Productivity

Productivity is on the tip of every manager's tongue these days. Unhappily for the politicians and others who constantly pontificate on the need to improve the level of productivity, human beings learn. They know that in a world where growth has slowed markedly, higher productivity levels generally imply fewer jobs, not more goods produced. This is the social dilemma. And when the work-force is asked to do more, each of them recognizes that this may mean that the next man on the shop floor will be out of a job or that he himself will not get the overtime. Obviously, this does not apply in fast-growing markets, but these are now the minority for developed Western economies. It is a 'behavioural' problem, which is as unlikely of fast solution as ironing out the trade cycle. This does not mean that individual activities cannot act, like Consumer Manufacturers, to automate and eliminate a sector of employees;

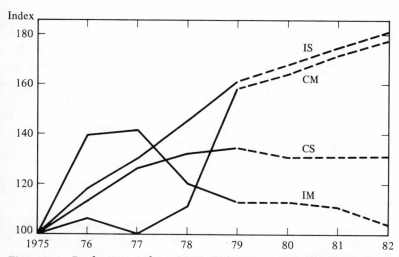

Figure 7.6 Productivity indices, 1975–82 (1975 = 100): IS, Industrial Services; CM, Consumer Manufacturers; CS, Consumer Services; IM, Industrial Manufacturers

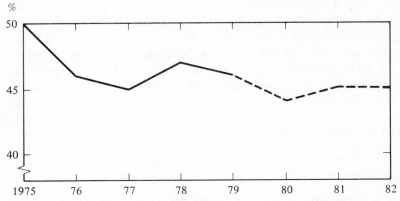

Figure 7.7   Employment costs/value added, 1975–82, Industrial Services

but it does signify that promises of major productivity improvements without such action are likely to be disappointed. So what are Conglom's Activities up to? Figure 7.6 which shows changes in productivity (or value added *per capita*) gives the story.

The graphs for value added *per capita*, deflated and indexed to 1975, indicate that Industrial Services was achieving a high 13 per cent per annum (compound) improvement, but expected this to abate to 9 per cent. This is still a high figure, but management has proved in the past that it can do it. The review of Industrial Services' employment costs as a proportion of value added in Fig. 7.7 indicates, too, that this is not at the cost of giving anything away in wages.

A lower trajectory is shown in Fig. 7.6 for Consumer Services value added *per capita*; at the beginning of the period, too, employment costs to value added reduce sharply. Until Consumer Manufacturers' streamlining move was implemented, productivity there was not improving materially. There was a step change in 1979. It is too early to judge, therefore, whether the prospective 8.5 per cent per annum is feasible.

Finally, Industrial Manufacturers are in the doldrums again, with a 3 per cent historical improvement and the future virtually static. And look how employment costs are creeping up (Fig. 7.8) as a percentage of value added!

Other costs

'Other costs'—i.e., the residuals—are not susceptible to a similar analytical approach. Additional expenses were incurred by Consumer Manufacturers on its streamlining, but these were one-off in 1979 and the plan shows a reversion to trend. The big chunk of extra cost in Industrial Manufacturers resulted from

90

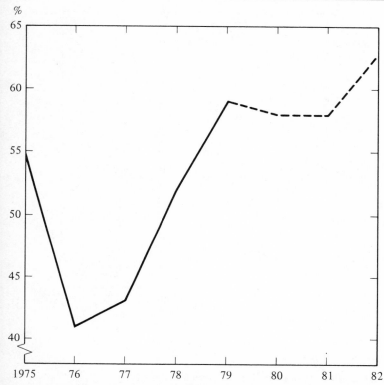

Figure 7.8 Employment costs/value added, 1975–82, Industrial Manufacturers

the move to new premises. This had been planned for some time, and certainly before the 1974 recession hit its markets. When, therefore, it managed to start up in the new factory just on the upside of the cycle, with volumes responding (admittedly, to a degree, sales were being sustained out of stocks), the managers felt they had got it right, even though there was a once-for-all increase in the level of cost. They appear to have admitted pretty soon after this, though, that they were in fact on a downward track. They sub-let a part of their premises in 1979 and have tried to contain costs. Their expectation for such a big drop in costs in 1982, however, looks like a balancing figure to solve an otherwise insoluble equation.

It may be misleading to assess individually the risks and uncertainties in these figures—not least because experience teaches that Fate is not dextrous enough to sling stones and shoot arrows simultaneously for more than short bursts. Nevertheless, to try to specify the range of uncertainty, we shall take an overview at the trading profit level.

91

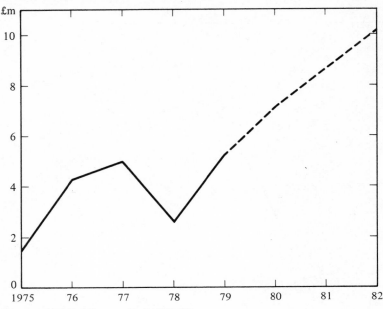

Figure 7.9 Trading profit, 1975–82

Trading profit

The profile of trading profit for the group is shown in Fig. 7.9. This does not look bad for 1975–77. There is a sudden drop in 1978 before it goes back up in 1979. Note that trading profit for Conglom includes 'Extraordinary' activity costs. After that it's roses all the way! Before dismissing the forecasts as a blindfold salesman's lunge into the future on a pogo stick, however, the underlying activities must again be examined. The Industrial Services profit margin seems achievable in 1980, but thereafter goes up by a half per cent per annum. This is higher than ever before and might be too testing a target, but it does emanate from the market stance described and would represent success. On the other hand, Consumer Services expects a reduced margin, which seems reasonable in the circumstances. Whether Consumer Manufacturers will pull off its move into profit is, of course, what corporate management is hoping and praying for. It had a big dip in 1978 as a result of consolidation of all its production facilities on one site. For safety's sake, a provision against a less dramatic margin improvement seems a sensible precaution to take. Finally, on Industrial Manufacturers, the other big problem area whose profits also reduced sharply in 1978, can the slide be halted and turned round as happened in 1976? Again, to assess the risk implicit in this situation, it would be wise to test for the implications of a static margin from now on at 2.3 per cent.

92

Table 7.1

Activity	Factor	Provision	Result		1980	1981	1982
Industrial Services	Price increase	Abate by 10 points each plan year	Sales	(£m)	21.5	24.8	27.7
	Margin	Hold at 1979 level	Margin	(%)	14·8	14·8	14·8
			Trading profit	(£m)	3·2	3·7	4·1
Consumer Services	Price increase	Abate by 10 points each plan year	Sales	(£m)	14·6	16·3	17·7
	Margin	As plan	Margin	(%)	12·8	13·4	13·6
			Trading profit	(£m)	1.9	2.2	2.4
Consumer Manufacturers	Margin	Slower recovery	Margin	(%)	0	3.6	6.9
			Trading profit	(£m)	0	0.3	0.7
Industrial Manufacturers	Margin	Hold at 1974 level	Margin	(%)	2.3	2.3	2.3
			Trading profit	(£m)	0.6	0.7	0.7

The full list of factors in respect of which the management of Conglom might wish to make some risk provision in view of the foregoing, could include those given in Table 7.1. Table 7.2 gives a total revised trading profit, compared with plan. The net effect of this would be a significant reduction in the trading profit even before we start considering the macro-environment. An alternative trajectory, therefore, based on the new assumptions proposed above would look like Fig. 7.10. This still shows an improving profit line, but it does take cognizance of a somewhat more difficult competitive and cost environment than in the base activity forecasts.

Table 7.2

		1980	1981	1982
Plan trading profit	(£m)	7.1	8.6	10.1
Revised trading profit	(£m)	5.7	6.9	7.9
Difference (provision)	(£m)	(1.4)	(1.7)	(2.2)

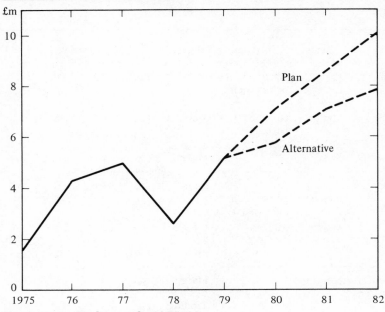

Figure 7.10   Trading profit, 1975–82

Working capital

Turning now to the investment side, what sort of projections have been made on working capital to sales ratios? The pattern of the past is the shape of a root symbol ($\sqrt{\ }$), as the 1976 recovery in sales shifted more inventory off the factory and warehouse floor (Fig. 7.11). Thereafter, control seems to have slipped somewhat, but the plan promises that it will be reasserted.

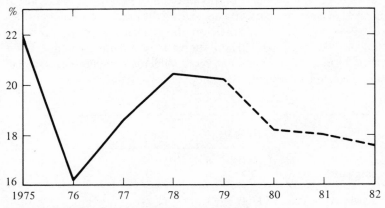

Figure 7.11   Working capital/sales, 1975–82

94

A more detailed activity analysis, however, shows who, specificity, is promising what. Industrial Services, for instance, is actually intending to increase the amount of working capital, as its ratio rises by 1 per cent in the plan year to a level significantly higher than ever before. There could be some over-provision here; in particular, the monetary working capital looks to be excessive and the implications of a higher credit policy needs to be pursued. The Consumer Services figures, while relatively high historically, seem, nevertheless, reasonable as a plan to move back to a lower level over three years. Again, better control on receivables may be the answer. A lower sales figure would, of course, reduce working capital. Consumer Manufacturers' working capital is mostly in inventories, and this jumps around. The proposals, however, are credible. It is, again, Industrial Manufacturers that is the problem. Admittedly, inventories dropped significantly as a proportion of sales in 1976, but since then they have moved up sharply. Any expectation, therefore, that a 5 per cent improvement can be achieved in one year seems over-optimistic. A more modest change should be tested. Since this activity carries the bulk of Conglom's working capital, such a revision is going to have a major impact on cash flow.

Fixed capital

Finally, there is the question of fixed capital expenditure. Industrial Services has had approval to overcome its capacity utilization problems. So now plant is being installed to remove bottlenecks and increase output. The Consumer Services business has a very low capital intensity, but is buying new computers. Since Consumer Manufacturers have been spending a fair amount in the recent past, the level of expenditure here has fallen. Perhaps the only area for concern is Industrial Manufacturers, where capital expenditure continually lies below the replacement depreciation costs—but capacity utilization is falling rapidly. Real courage, backed by conviction of managerial ability to stem the trend, would be needed. In its absence, the downward sales spiral is exacerbated by ageing equipment's producing poorer quality goods. On balance, no test changes are proposed in capital expenditure.

Trading cash flow

So now all the components of trading cash flow are assembled. Working capital is subject to change, as can be seen in Table 7.3. To this we add the change in trading profit to give an alternative trading cash flow compared with plan (Table 7.4). The base forecast with the impact of the revisions on cash flow is given in Figure 7.12.

Looking now at the cash flow after interest, tax, and dividends, the position is more doubtful. The last three years (including the current one) have

95

Table 7.3

Activity	Provision	1980	Result 1981	1982
		£m	£m	£m
Industrial Services	Reduced sales as above	0.6	0.6	0.6
Consumer Services	Reduced sales as above	0.0	0.1	0.1
Industrial Manufacturers	Raise ratios to 31%, 30%, and 29% for 3 plan years	(0.9)	(0.9)	(0.6)
	Net effect on trading cash flow	(0.3)	(0.2)	0.1

Table 7.4

	1980	1981	1982
	£m	£m	£m
Plan trading cash flow	5.2	6.7	8.1
Revised trading cash flow	3.5	4.8	6.0
Difference (provision)	1.7	1.9	2.1

produced a cash outflow of £5 million. In providing for increased long-term borrowings and a rise in dividends in the plan (see Schedule 2), there has to be an expectation of improved results to enable such financial policies to be implemented. The revised trading cash flow projections are likely, however, to result in the figures shown in Table 7.5. The overall recovery in the financial position of the organization is significantly postponed.

This is the operational uncertainty perceived in the plans, as measured by the departure from base-case cash flow. Again, we emphasize that this is calculated by reference to the plan Base-Case assumptions, before seeing how alternative economic, political, social, or any other macro-factors will pull it apart. We have gone through this exercise to demonstrate the way in which a change in any item can produce change in the corporate results. We did not, in fact, use the financial models to do this. While it is clear that we can make these sorts of adjustments for a four-activity business by hand (so long as we have calculators and a wet towel), when we move into more than this, and look at the environmental strategies and financing constraints and make choices, it

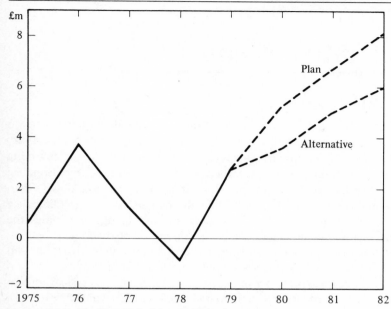

Figure 7.12   Trading cash flow, 1975–82

Table 7.5

	1980	1981	1982
Plan total cash flow (£m)	3.1	3.6	3.0
Revised total cash flow (£m)	1.1	1.8	1.4
Plan debt (£m)	9.2	5.6	2.6
Revised debt (£m)	11.2	9.4	8.0
Plan D/E ratio (%)	47	25	9
Revised D/E ratio (%)	60	46	34

becomes an impossible task except with a machine. By arranging to input alternative views of sales volumes and prices, working capital ratios and fixed capital expenditure, the corporate financial model will undertake all the calculations contained in the foregoing review and produce revised P & L accounts, cash flow statements, and balance sheets. Thus the whole spectrum of accounting measures can be compared with the original plan statistics and decisions made about where to apply the pressure managerially.

97

8.
Alternative scenarios

Wild cards in the forecasting pack

Any forecast will have its 'wild cards'. Time and time again, forecasters, in setting their residuals and input values, will be making conditional assumptions.[1] Some set of assumptions is adopted and the impact modelled: 'assuming government policy does not change, then these input values seem reasonable; assuming the labour force accepts that inflation is coming down, then residuals on the wage equations will follow this course; assuming OPEC policy is unchanged, oil prices will take this value'; and so on. Sometimes the equations themselves are inadequate, or differences of theoretical opinion admit several interpretations of events, so there can be quite a wide discretion in setting residuals. In such cases the forecaster will be assuming a certain theoretical structure to prevail over alternatives. Each conditional assumption represents a 'wild card'; if some of them had a different face value, the model's predictions could be quite different. The essence of scenario planning is to identify the important wild cards and play them.

The justification for examining these wild cards is, therefore, self-evident. There are a variety of possible futures that can be foreseen. If a business is drawing up plans on the basis of one of these possible futures, management can hardly be indifferent to the fact that there are alternatives around which could imply going broke—or getting rich. Plans must contain enough room for manoeuvre, such that if the environment does turn out markedly different, the business can still progress towards its objectives. Effective leadership requires simple clear-cut aims to be set. If management chooses to take a leaf out of the Duke of York's book and lead the men up the hill and then they have to come down again, because management did not consider the alternatives that lay beyond the crest, this will soon create a dispirited force. The aim should be to design plans that appear robust against an uncertain, but explored, future, so that any change in the environment produces at most a change in emphasis in priorities, and not a complete U-Turn.

Choosing scenarios

How, then, are alternative scenarios to be chosen? Any exploration into space starts with people; in consequence, views of the future are limited only by the planner's imagination. The exercise starts with the judgement and selectivity of the scenario designer. It requires in this person a sensitivity to the social, political, and economic environments in which the corporation finds itself.

Some people are very skilled at discerning trends and forces at work within a society or the international community; this skill will normally be supported by a very wide reading and thinking (an underrated pastime because of its overt lack of activity), in order continuously to monitor the ebbs and flows of the external scene. Allowing the fertility of an informed mind, therefore, the potentially infinite range must be cut down to a manageable number of scenarios.

There are certain criteria that can be brought to bear in the selection process. The starting point must be the perceived vulnerabilities or exposure of the company concerned. This is where the various micro-models and linkages are helpful, since they embody those macroeconomic influences that systematically affect the markets and trading environment of the company. A business may be heavily exposed to the vagaries of consumer durable expenditure or perhaps to manufacturing output. Although an assumed change of any economic significance to the base-case will eventually influence most sectors of the economy, it may affect one sector first and to a far greater extent than others.

For instance, at the time of writing, the UK economy is suffering an inordinately large deterioration in competitiveness. The main impact centres on the manufacturing sector. Consumer spending will, in due course, be affected, but the initial shock comes from the squeeze on manufacturers. In 1978/79 wages were able to grow faster than consumer prices for a significant period, and as a result consumer spending, particularly on durables, rose significantly. The benefits were not passed on to the manufacturing sector to the full extent, because demand was met from imports. Manufacturers were the ones who suffered first and worst.

The cost structure of a company also reveals its vulnerability. A business might have high energy or commodity costs, and therefore be vulnerable to large increases in price. The situation could become very uncomfortable if costs could not be passed on to customers. Suppose, as is currently the case, that US industry were enjoying oil costs below world prices. UK competitors in products with high oil-based content (e.g., man-made fibres), and in competition with the USA, might not be able to put up prices to cover their rising and greater costs. The result would be a squeeze on UK margins. Similarly, labour costs are another area where rapid increases might not be easy to pass on, depending on the exchange rate, and this, therefore, would also produce a margin squeeze.

As far as cash is concerned, besides the inventory consequences of rapid changes in demand, exposure to foreign exchange risk on overseas debts can be important for some companies. If this is the case, the scenarios that involve falls in the domestic currency would be worth considering. A corporation might be caught in a hard currency trap, having borrowed from a strong currency source to finance operations in a weak currency

99

area. A scenario could be used to spring that trap to underline the possible exposure.

Classes of scenarios

So it is clear that a feeling for the structural vulnerabilities of the corporation is an important starting point in the scenario-designing exercise. Scenarios whose impacts are likely to be on those economic aggregates upon which the corporation is most dependant become almost self-selecting. However, scenarios can suggest themselves in various ways. For instance, when the new forecast or simulation base is being developed on the macro-model, many of the conditional assumptions are unavoidably confronted. The structure of the model obliges the user to make assumptions, not only in setting the input values, but in setting the paths of residuals. The forecast or scenario is conditional upon these assumptions. They might be about raw material prices, about governmental policy, or about responses of various sectors to recent and unusual shocks. Thus the very activity of producing a new forecast can suggest alternative scenarios. Typically, two sorts do emerge; one based on purely technical considerations, and another that is more substantive. The dividing line is not sharp.

A technical scenario may arise from a combination of the limitations of the model and the reasonable expectations of the user. In the Base-Case quoted in Chapter 6 we generated a new forecast, where, in the early years, a deep recession was produced contemporaneously with a chronic deterioration in competitiveness. Wages began to fall and interest rates came down, producing conditions for a recovery. Using a particular model, the investment recovery was very strong, and, because rapid growth did not raise inflation (owing to the formulation of the price and wage equations), was sustained. However, a counter-argument could be made that recovery, at least in the UK, quickly runs into bottlenecks, and that not only would investment grow less slowly, but inflation would pick up. Furthermore, given the competitive squeeze that preceded the recovery, many firms might be tempted to invest abroad to spread their risk. If that were to occur, then some of the investment being forecast for the UK would actually be going abroad and not raising economic activity domestically. Thus, raising prices and lowering investment residuals in the recovery phase to reflect these possibilities could produce a quite different picture. In fact, this was a real example of a set of scenarios used in a recent planning round, in which various recovery options were tested. These adjustments might be said to form a purely technical scenario.

Just as producing a new forecast raises possible technical scenarios, so can more substantive scenarios be provoked. When the user is setting his raw material prices for a forecast he may take the view that the conditions in the metal markets and in the producer areas—perhaps southern Africa—do not

100

suggest an imminent price hike of 1973/74 proportions. This is his best guess. However, the politics of the area are volatile, and five minutes' thought could suggest several combinations of events that could produce a large increase in spot and contract rates. It is less important to be precise about the possible events than to make decisions about the amount by which these prices might be increased. Naturally this would vary with circumstances; for a mining company the differences could be critical, and would form part of its market scenario, but ultimately a judgement must be made. It may not be an entirely correct decision, but it at least admits the possibility that the assumption is open to debate and that the implications are worth explaining. Scenarios explore the potential risk.

Other scenario sources

Government policy is another major scenario source. The base-case forecast is normally based on unchanged government policies, certainly for the later years. Changes in policy, perhaps as a response to the situation apparently emerging from the new forecast, can then be attempted. On unchanged policies, the economy may be plunging into a very deep recession, and political pressures would be mounting for some restimulation in the later years. Scenarios could investigate this possibility.

They may also be used to delve into changing economic fashions. Another example of a quite radical approach—at least, it was some years ago when we first designed it—was the use of a strict UK monetary policy to curb a wages explosion. This scenario was prompted by the shift in intellectual opinion that was occurring and was beginning to be taken seriously by government circles. This change of opinion was apparent from following the financial press. What was unclear, at least to some, was the effect it would have on the economy.

A related aspect that can be reviewed with scenarios is the manner in which a policy might work out. The Thatcher monetary experiment has divided economic opinion.[2] Some economists see a money squeeze working directly on reducing inflation without much loss of output; others see precisely the reverse. Proponents argue that there would be behavioural changes in certain areas, primarily in wage bargaining, such that macro-models based on historic relationships would cease to be valid. A scenario-designer can exogenize the wage equation so that it produces the expectations of the proponents and so can explore the uncertainty.

Probability and impact

The formulation of scenarios is therefore assisted by an appreciation of company vulnerabilities and by actually working with the macro-model to produce a revised new forecast. The latter confronts the user with the

101

conditional assumptions that could be changed in a scenario. Now, although scenarios will suggest themselves, certain guiding principles are still required. A balance must be struck along two scales: one is proability, the other is magnitude of impact. They are not entirely independent. Management might view with total equanimity the development of a highly probable event with a low impact while being very concerned about a low-probability event with a high impact. The tendency is to concentrate a good deal of effort in establishing probabilities using simple guesswork or some sort of sophisticated Delphi technique.

There are, however, some severe problems in determining numerical probabilities. A scenario will normally be characterized by an assumed, well-defined, event. Although such events could be ranked on a probability basis (perhaps even given probability ratings), the manner in which that event is treated by the planner on the macro-model is germane to assessing the likelihood of the scenario. It is important to distinguish between the probability of the impact—e.g., oil price rising in real terms by 35 per cent in 1985—and

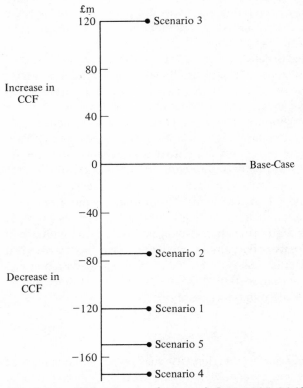

Figure 8.1   Change in cumulative cash flow, 1985–86 (£m)

102

the probability of subsequent events working out in the manner suggested by the model. If the consequences predicted by the model can be taken on faith, then the problem of setting probabilities reduces to guaging the likelihood of the impact.

The impact of any scenario, once it has been simulated, can be measured directly from the cash flow it generates or more particularly by its deviation from base. Figure 8.1 illustrates a variety of deviations from base plan by 1985/86. This form of presentation shows that, by 1985/86, scenario 4 has produced an adverse movement of £180m in cumulative cash flow with respect to Base-Case. It might be tempting to call this the 'worst' scenario— indeed, it is unavoidable that managers will apply these terms to the scenarios. However, this would ignore the time profile.

While it may be interesting to know which scenario bankrupts a company by the end of the plan period on unchanged strategies, it is essential to know whether any result in catastrophe before the plan ends. Figure 8.2 shows only three scenarios, all consistent with Fig. 8.1. Scenario 3 is undoubtely the best of the bunch, but is scenario 4 worse than scenario 1? This problem is ultimately one of classification, but it does not matter which is labelled 'worse'

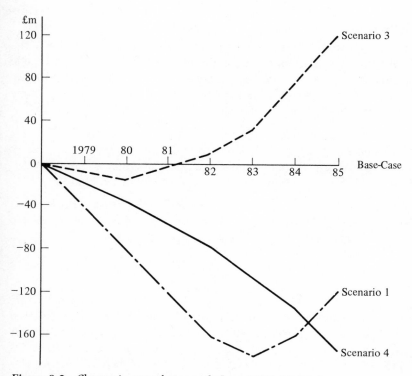

Figure 8.2   Change in cumulative cash flow, 1979–85 (£m)

providing that the managers are alive to the implications of the different time profiles. In this way, reasonable guidance on the relative impact of the different scenarios may be obtained, the best and worst conditions identified, and a range within which to plan established. Once the scenario-planner has become familiar with his models and their simulation properties, he can gauge the likely consequences of scenarios, in terms of very broad magnitudes sufficient to weed out the inconsequential from the insignificant.

In the four years that we have operated this system of alternative futures, some scenarios have become favourites in the sense that they recur frequently, while others have risen and fallen with the prevailing conventional wisdom. Some are global, but these are numerically fewer, while the remainder are national scenarios with particular attention being paid to the UK, where most of our businesses are based. In some cases national scenarios have been imposed upon global scenarios. The number of scenarios prepared in any one year for the purposes of the plan, has ranged between five and ten. This falls far short of being exhaustive; but, as will become apparent, with careful design the scenarios can, and indeed have, captured the more dramatic economic developments.

Oil scenarios

Among the list of firm favourites has been the possibility of a repetition of the 1974 oil price hike. The rationale for the price of oil rising by a dramatic amount in real terms has always been firmly rooted in the politics of the Middle East. The crisis has been seen as possibly being unleashed by one of three developments, although others may be readily imagined:

- increased tension, including war between Arabs and Israelis
- Gulf feud breaking out into a hot war (Iran–Iraq)
- change in pricing policies of Saudis as a result of either a change in the ruling establishment or from a simple reassessment of self-interest

For those in the oil business, these become industry scenarios rather than global macroeconomic conditions. However, for many other economic participants there are really only two questions to be answered:

- when?
- how much?

They are not unrelated questions, and depend to some extent on which of the three causes is being envisaged. In preparing the simulation, it was assumed that increases of 25–30 per cent would occur in the real price of oil. Timing has varied from one to two years out from the date of preparation. Probabilities have varied also, but this is not important at this stage. The deriving of a proposed increase was based, within limits, upon econometric techniques that explored the global demand and supply balance. To some extent the state of demand, i.e., whether the Western economies are booming or in recession, was expected to have a great bearing on price sensitivity to supply change. However, at the end of the day judgements had to be supplied on both the amount and timing in the light of what was said about probability and impact.

The difference between the Base-Case scenario adopted for 1980 and an oil crisis scenario, which assumed a real rise of 30 per cent in 1981, is effectively depicted in Fig. 8.3 in the UK and US GDP growth curves. Translated into specific terms, there are major changes on a number of macro-factors, as can be seen in Table 8.1.

Table 8.1

	United Kingdom						USA			
	Base-case			Oil crisis*			Base-case		Oil crisis	
	GDP	WPI	$/£	GDP	WPI	$/£	GNP	WPI	GNP	WPI
	%	%	%	%	%	%	%	%	%	%
1980	−0.5	10·3	2.20	−3.4	12.5	2.33	−0.5	10.7	−0.8	15.4
1981	1.9	10.3	2.15	−2.8	15.0	2.39	3.4	8.5	−0.4	14.1
1982	4.0	9.4	2.06	3.0	9.4	2.45	2.4	8.5	0.7	12.1
1983	5.3	8.3	1.06	6.8	5.1	2.51	3.6	8.5	3.2	9.9
1984	4.3	13.0	2.06	6.6	6.4	2.60	2.3	9.4	4.3	9.7
1985	2.7	12.0	2.06	1.7	6.5	2.65	2.7	10.2	4.6	0.3

* based on new simulation case (see Table 6.3).

Once the timing and the amount of increase was settled, some assumptions were required about government actions. The main issue was whether they would take measures to restrain internal demand and by how much. Only the interpretation of recent history could be a guide in this matter. At the time of the second oil increase in 1979/80, which was very much larger than the 30 per cent increase actually assumed in previous oil scenarios, it was apparent that many countries would seek to follow 'beggar-my-neighbour' exchange rate policies by squeezing their monetary base and so forcing up interest rates. A judgement was made, therefore, on how much interest rates might rise and the policy component of the fiscal deficit be cut.

A variety of factors influence the policy response. If the economy is very depressed, measures to depress it further will be tempered by the social and political implications. The strength of the government to carry through unpopular deflationary policies will have an important bearing on the policy response adopted. Furthermore some countries will be larger oil importers than others, and consequently the balance of payments implications could be far more serious, requiring a firmer policy. These influences must be given their weight and a judgement made on them by the scenario-planner. (If it is

GDP UK

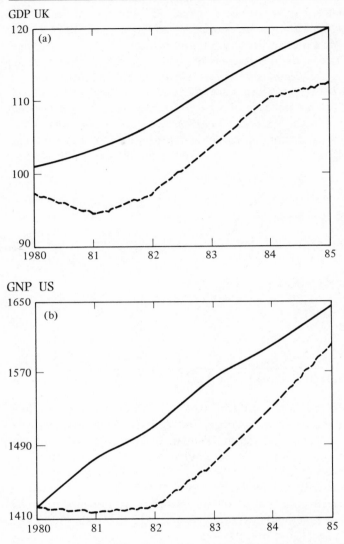

GNP US

Figure 8.3   (a) UK GDP, oil crisis (1975 prices, £bn); (b) US GNP oil crisis (1972 prices, $bn). Base-case, solid line; oil scenario, broken line

any consolation, it is just as difficult for the luckless government to make the same decision, and it is having to do it in the real world, not a duplicate.)

Other global scenarios

Other global scenarios have sought to assess the chances of the USA, Germany, and Japan, 'locomotives' of the Western world, successfully leading it out of

106

recession, given known national concerns on inflation rates and balance of payments deficits. This was very much a live issue in 1977, with world leaders seeking to invoke their neighbours to take a risky course, while remaining poised to jump on their coat-tails if everything went well. The scenario that was developed showed that, within the political constraints acting upon the major participants, not a lot could be expected. This also proved to be the case in the real world.

In this scenario it was assumed that the reflators would not be prepared to see more than a certain amount of inflation in their respective economies, or too dramatic a swing in either their balance of payments or exchange rates. The policy component of the fiscal deficit was increased (see Chapter 5) in each country, until such time as the economy began to move into the assumed danger zones. The judgement on where these danger zones lay required not only an appreciation of the current political scene in each country, particularly with respect to economic issues, but also the economic history of the countries. Immediate access to economic data bases going back two or three decades can be very useful, since it provides a quantitative view of the past, which with care can be read for such things as the tolerances of the local populace. Italians and Britons are demonstrably more tolerant of inflation than their German counterparts. Seven or 8 per cent inflation in Germany would currently be a serious political matter for people who still remember hyperinflation and the disastrous political sequel, whereas in both Italy and the UK this is a rate to which they would at present aspire. Fortunately, most computer-based macro-models will have such data bases for an immediate inspection of historical statistics.

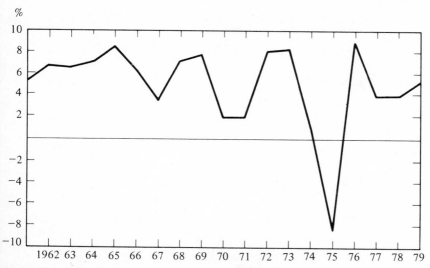

Figure 8.4 Growth in OECD industrial production, 1962–79

A third global scenario that has been repeated on numerous occasions is not unrelated to the previous one. Following the 1973/74 oil crisis, most countries have achieved a much slower growth rate in both output and productivity (see Fig. 8.4), so much so that some economists have suggested that the calendar should be rebased: instead of 1974 AD, one would now write 1 AO (After OPEC). Although each country has been affected to a different degree, most developed countries are growing more slowly, and it would seem to be as a result of a structural response to the change in energy prices. It has taken some time for this to be widely recognized; the poor economic performance after OPEC was assumed to be a temporary aberration. Without pretending to explain the precise forces that have given rise to this deterioration, scenarios were devised that reflected continued low world growth.

National scenarios

Most of our national scenarios have, inevitably, been for the UK, although some were 'inflicted' upon the USA, Canada, and the Netherlands. Although the non-UK scenarios have varied in detail, they have tended to be 'technical' scenarios, in the sense described earlier. If growth were seen to be turning down in one of these countries and there were economists who claimed that the situation might indeed be more serious than most forecasts suggested, then a recession scenario might be tried. Similarly, if there existed a particularly wide spread of opinion on prospective rates of inflation, a high-inflation scenario would be designed. Occasionally more profound structural problems would be assessed over the medium term.

In 1978 a prolonged stagflationary scenario was considered for the USA.

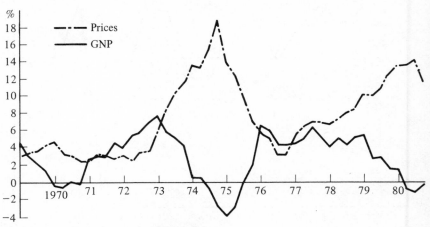

Figure 8.5   US output and prices, 1970–80

108

This was provoked by concern over quite well established trends to both slower growth and higher inflation (see Fig. 8.5). The scenario was, therefore, based on a veiw that the USA, as a whole, had lost a great deal of its economic dynamism of the 1960s, and the oil crisis both disguised and aggravated the deterioration. The post-oil crisis performance was seen not exclusively as a response to higher oil prices, but also as owing to an underlying decline (see Fig. 8.6). In the scenario, productivity growth was constrained and inflation remained relatively high. US policy-makers were seen battling with a severe problem of high levels of unemployment, which, if it sought to correct with injections of demand, resulted in an acceleration in inflation. The dilemma was never resolved in the scenario, and so there was simultaneous stagnation and relatively high inflation. The dollar went into a steady decline. It was the sort of muddling-through scenario that a British audience would find easy to understand.

A Dutch scenario addressed what has been referred to as the 'Dutch disease'. This ailment manifests itself in a strong currency which does not fully adjust for differential inflation rates and so produces a trade squeeze on domestic producers. The reason for the intransigent exchange rate is that

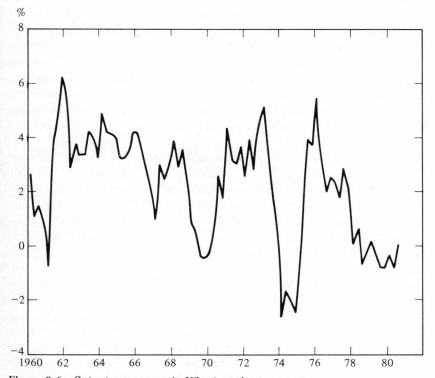

Figure 8.6 Output per person, in US private business sector

109

Holland is rich in gas supplies and exports a significant proportion. This gives it a relatively strong underlying balance of payments on current account, boosted each time the relative cost of energy rises. The guilder, therefore, tends to remain strong, a little too strong for some manufacturers. The scenario imagined circumstances under which the Dutch disease might turn malignant. The level of uncompetitiveness was raised further, and intensified the incipient squeeze on manufacturers.

UK scenarios

On the whole, UK scenarios have been concerned with two major and not always unrelated themes. The first has been the impact of North Sea oil on the UK economy, and the second, government policy in the face of high prices and wages inflation. Early scenarios, which anticipated the UK catching a dose of the Dutch disease as a result of North Sea oil output, assumed a variety of policy responses. For instance, in 1978, taking account of the influence of North Sea oil on government revenues and the current account balance of payments, it was assumed that the government might pursue a policy of expansion while simultaneously taking measures to reduce the value of the pound. Measures envisaged were a relaxation of exchange controls, more Third World aid, and the financing of less national debt overseas. The aim would be to stimulate net capital account outflows to compensate for the positive effect on sterling of an oil-induced current account surplus. The critical assumption was that the government could actually operate successfully on the capital account. The result was fairly good growth. A variant of this scenario saw the situation of cuts in taxes producing massive imports on current account and deferring the period of strong balance of payments and the strong pound.

As was mentioned earlier, one of the favourites among the UK scenarios was an attempt to contain a wage explosion using monetary control. Our exercise in May 1978 had certain prophetic qualities, inasmuch as it assumed a wage surge of 20 per cent and sterling M3 targets of 11–13 per cent. The consequence was a drastic fall in output, with inflation reducing only slowly. Once this began to move from the realms of possibility to a nightmarish reality, a great deal of attention was focused on the possible variants of the high wage–tight money scenario. In 1979 a set of scenarios was designed, collectively entitled 'The Monetary Mystery Tour', to explore the consequences of the new government's declared policy. There were three versions. The first had a prolonged squeeze on the economy producing a slump in output and inflation moderating slowly. The government envisaged behaviour changing and wage settlements moderating quickly, such that any squeeze on the corporate sector would be short-lived. And it pursued its policies to the bitter end. The results were inevitably depressing, with GDP falling 2–3 per cent in a

110

year and unemployment to 1930 levels, because the model, like most models, did not embody the same rationale or theoretical views as the government propounded. In fact, it behaved with almost human stubbornness. The second version imposed the view of the government on the model, and wages were brought down dramatically. The third version saw not a change in behaviour, but a change in government policy (a U-turn). Although a variety of alternative policy options were conceivable, the one actually chosen was a reflation of the economy and a relaxation of monetary control.

As was to be expected, neither in the first case of intransigence all round, nor in the last, where government went back on the old track of palliatives—suppressing the symptoms and not the causes—was there any material improvement in economic health. Only where there was a real wage drop did investment-led recovery emerge.

Limitations on scenario planning

These scenarios illustrate the strengths of the approach. They were flagging that a potentially serious situation might develop in the following years. They showed the direction and shape of the trend. The cash implications for corporations operating in such an environment were manifestly severe. Despite some good guesses, they also illustrate that precision is not possible:

- First, it is impractical to interpret the cash flow change as anything more than impressionistic.
- Second, events did not quite turn out as any single scenario suggested.

In fact, what occurred in 1980 was a combination of a high oil price rise (greater than assumed even in our worst case oil scenario), with all its implications for sterling, and a government pursuing a tight monetary policy.

Various scenarios can be combined. Unfortunately, it is not possible simply to add the impact of the different outcomes together. In some cases the resultant effect upon economic aggregates would imply a significantly worse climate in which failure by government to act would be inconceivable. In others, the impact of certain events could be self-cancelling, so the coincidence of events would not lead to a materially worse situation. It would be unrealistic to try all combinations, so the rule should be to test the simultaneous occurrence only of those scenarios that suggest the most significant impact and whose individual probabilities are high and not mutually exclusive.

Equally, it would be unrealistic to assume that the budget for undertaking simulations was unlimited. While the experienced operator can do much to minimize his processing costs, they are not inexpensive. It can cost anything between £5000 and £10 000 at the present time to run through half a dozen scenarios and assemble them in a fit state for the corporate plan. And there is no assurance, at times, in moments of planning panic, that any results will be

111

obtained by the time-table deadline! However, if the exercise can be spread over a reasonable period, then there is the possibility of taking advantage of deferred run discounts. Computer agencies give substantial discounts to time-sharers if they are prepared to schedule their use of computing during non-peak periods, i.e., at weekends and overnight. This does not mean that the users have to work then, but merely that a run is queued until that time.

Given all the practical and theoretical limitations, it is clear, nevertheless, that the system will give useful indications of the way in which the business is likely to react to possible changes in the environment. In selecting scenarios, the planner, in partnership with managers, will steer a line between impact and probability. With experience he will be able to guess very roughly in advance the impact of a scenario to be simulated by his models. At the end, he will be able to gauge its *relative* gravity. He will also have an opinion about its probability. There is little point in putting through scenarios with minimal impact, and this often rules out many, though not all, of the purely technical scenarios that suggest themselves. At the other end of the scale, he should also avoid simulating, say, the remote possibility of energy at $1 per barrel. And he must also ignore the lure of the Armageddon scenario, where the impact would be so severe as to negate the validity of corporate existence: there is no point in housing the accounts in nuclear-proof shelters or in fussing about debt/equity ratio, post the red revolution.

Notes

1. P. Ormerod, *The Limits to Economic Forecasting*, Labour Economic Finance and Taxation Association, London, pp. 2–6.
2. For policy statement, see *Financial Statement and Budget Report, 1980–81*, HMSO, London, 1980. For criticism, see 'Third Report from the Treasury and Civil Service Committee, Session 1980–81', *Monetary Policy*, vol. 1, House of Commons, London, 24 February 1981.

9.
Crisis at Conglom

An alternative scenario

We come now to the final act of our economic odyssey. In it we shall take the Base-Case upon which Conglom's results were prepared and manipulate these through a rise in the real price of oil, showing the route as we go, the results it engenders, and the way in which Conglom's management might react to it. While this is an exercise carried out in a duplicate world, it remains valid as a way of looking at the environment in the real world and arriving at strategies that are robust to the external turbulence to which managers are becoming accustomed. It would be possible to simulate several scenarios, but for the sake of exposition the exercise is limited to one. We shall adopt, wholesale for this purpose, the revised assumptions on oil prices referred to in Chapter 8.

The linkages

Each of the businesses has a micro-model, which requires macroeconomic inputs to generate future market values such as prices and sales. For Consumer Services Ltd the price of its products is determined by labour costs and raw material prices in a simple mark-up theory of price-setting. The surge in inflation resulting from the oil prince hike pushes up wages over the Base-Case, tending to raise activity prices. (The Base-Case was the basis of the businesses' plans while the scenario was simulated from a revised base, which took into account the prospective deterioration in output and higher inflation that had become apparent since the guidelines were issued.) Raw material costs, though technically exogenous, have been found to be a function not only of labour costs in the UK but of overseas commodity prices, which, *inter alia*, depend on the exchange rate. The value of sterling is boosted relative to the Base-Case primarily because of the capital account effect enjoyed by a petro-currency. This tends to mitigate the increase in Consumer Services' prices attributable to rises in sterling commodity prices. In the year of the oil price shock Consumer Services' prices are 17 per cent higher than base. The number of products sold is adversely affected by a rise in the price relative to the consumer price index, and, since consumer prices rose in 1981 by just under 17 per cent, a slight decline in sales volume will result. The volume of sales also rises with consumer expenditure, but unfortunately for Consumer Services, this is approximately 6 per cent down on the Base-Case. Part of the decline is due to the oil scenario; the remainder is the effect of the revision to Base. These market parameters are then fed into the financial model along with average earnings, exchange rates, etc.

Industrial Services Ltd manufactures packaging materials. The price and volume equations are given in functional form as:

$$P_{is} = f(W, IW)$$
$$V_{is} = f(P_{is}/WPI, IND)$$

where P_{is} is the wholesale price index of Industrial Services products, W is labour costs, IW is cost of imported materials, WPI is the UK wholesale price index, and IND is UK manufacturing output. The price of products rises with the UK labour costs and the cost of imported materials, the latter depending, *inter alia*, on the value of sterling. The price is up only 3 per cent in the year of the oil crisis, owing primarily to the depressed state of raw material prices, particularly in terms of sterling. Given that UK wholesale prices are up 13 per cent, the relative price term contributes substantially to volume sales (V_{is}). However, a near 15 per cent drop in manufacturing output decimates this favourable influence and causes output to drop some 25 per cent in the year of the oil crisis, relative to Base. The volume consequences, when fed through to the financial model, are quite severe for Industrial Services Ltd's profitability.

Consumer Manufacturerers BV are Dutch manufacturers selling both at home and abroad in a highly competitive market. The model embraces five countries: Italy, France, Germany, Belgium, and the Netherlands. For each country there is a production–consumption identity matrix:

Consumption (C) = Home sales by domestic producers (HS) + Imports (M)

Production (O) = Home sales by domestic producers (HS) + Exports (X)

Each country model seeks to explain consumption, market share (M/C), and exports. A price equation is also needed. The price equations are of the form:

$$P_D = f(L_D, L_F)$$

where L is labour costs and subscript D denotes domestic while F means foreign. This formulation sees domestic prices reflecting home and foreign levels of competitiveness. Consumption is a function of relative prices, consumer demand, and dwellings completed:

$$C_D = f(P_D/CPI_D, Con_D, D_D)$$

where C_D is consumption, CPI_D is domestic consumer prices, Con_D is consumer expenditure and D_D is dwellings completed. A rise in relative price depresses consumption, but will grow with increases in the other two explanatory variables.

The import share (M/C_D) is a function of relative unit labour costs R_L and a

114

pressure of demand variable CP_D, which is based on deviations from trend. The more uncompetitive the country becomes, the greater the market share that is lost. However, this can be exacerbated during periods of great demand when domestic producers have problems coping:

$$M/C_D = f(R_L, CP_D).$$

Finally, exports are a function of aggregate consumption abroad, C_F, and relative labour costs, R_L. During period of growing European consumption, exports rise but the relative growth rates in exports depend on competitiveness:

$$X_D = f(C_F, R_L).$$

These equations are enough to complete the rest of the production and consumption identities. The model is larger than the rest, largely because the market is open to trade, which is less the case in the previous two models. On the whole, the model reacts to the oil scenario by reducing consumption and hence trade but redistributes international market shares according to competitiveness.

The final company in Conglom, Industrial Manufacturers Ltd, is a maker of trucks, and the model used here is one developed by Economic Models Ltd. Not all models have to be home-made; it is quite possible to contract out the entire operation, and most agencies hiring macro-models will be more than keen to tender for such work for which they are uniquely qualified. Like all contracts, it is as well to have someone on your side who is as familiar with the techniques as the specialists to ensure value for money. The model provides only a volume measurement of the change in the light vans parc (stock of vehicles), and is a function of real disposable income and the real price of fuel. The oil crisis, therefore, hits the manufacture of vans doubly hard by reducing real disposable income and raising the real price of fuel.

The logic tree

The information on demand and other economic factors flows thereafter through the structure, depicted in Fig. 9.1. The logic tree shows how the changes in macroeconomic variables, such as exchange rates and interest rates, and micro-variables, such as volume, sales prices, and unit costs, ripple through the financial model. Changes in volumes and prices represent the stone pitched into the pool, whereafter the shock waves are felt by the rest of the financial system. Transmission is either via behavioural assumptions or accounting identities, both of which were described in Chapter 2.

Tracing the changes

The Base-Case forecasts for Conglom are summarized in Table 9.1. Whereas in

115

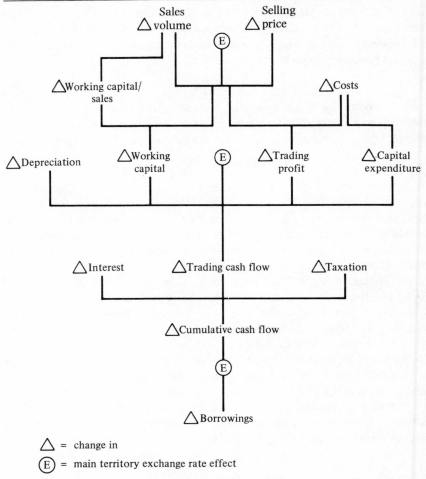

△ = change in

Ⓔ = main territory exchange rate effect

Figure 9.1 Logic tree of scenario analysis of changes

previous chapters attention was focused on the early years, in order to probe the more imminent commitments and judge the basic credibility of the businesses' plans, for the purposes of scenarios the full range of the plan must be considered. This allows the dynamics in the model to have full play.

In the oil crisis scenario to be demonstrated, the exchange rate effect resulting from the Dutch investment is taken into account in each row of changes, rather than as a separate item, so no figures show up specifically for this. Starting with sales, therefore, the consolidated effect of the macro-assumption changes, as predicted by the market models, and analysed by alterations in volume and price, is as given in Table 9.2. Trading profit can also be analysed into two broad effects producing the change between scenario and

Table 9.1

	1980	1981	1982	1983	1984	1985
	£m	£m	£m	£m	£m	£m
Total sales	76.6	84.4	90.7	99.7	109.0	119.0
Trading profit	7.1	8.6	10.1	11.2	12.2	13.3
Profit after tax	4.2	4.2	5.9	5.3	6.1	6.7
Depreciation	1.6	1.8	2.2	2.7	3.2	3.9
Capital expenditure	3.1	2.6	3.4	4.6	5.4	6.1
Trading cash flow	5.2	6.7	8.1	7.8	8.4	9.3
Total cash flow	3.1	3.6	3.0	2.6	2.7	3.5
Cumulative cash flow from 1979	3.1	6.7	9.7	12.3	15.0	18.5
Fixed assets at NBV	16.5	17.3	18.5	20.4	22.6	24.8
Working capital	13.9	15.0	15.8	17.5	19.3	21.2
Net equity	19.5	22.7	27.6	32.9	39.0	45.7
Total borrowings	9.2	5.6	2.6	0.0	(2.6)	(5.3)

Table 9.2

	1980	1981	1982	1983	1984	1985
	£m	£m	£m	£m	£m	£m
Base total sales	76.6	84.4	90.7	99.7	109.0	119.0
Volume effect of scenario	(3.9)	(15.6)	(14.0)	(10.9)	(10.2)	(14.5)
Price effect of scenario	2.6	5.8	5.7	4.3	(0.1)	(0.8)
Scenario total sales	75.3	74.6	82.4	93.1	98.7	103.7

base-cases. In this scenario, by far the largest factor accounting for a decline in profitability is the adverse movement in the cost structure, while the change in sales has had a relatively modest effect (Table 9.3). The consequences for working capital in this case are not radically different, because, though lower sales imply less financing, the adverse change in the working capital to sales ratio has nearly offset this effect (Table 9.4). Trading cash flow, in consequence of the foregoing and of alterations to fixed capital expenditure, which was lifted in line with changes in inflation and depreciation (which is a function of the values of fixed assets), takes the values set out in Table 9.5. The difference between the Base-Case and scenario cash flow then accumulates to the amounts shown in row 2 of Table 9.6, after adjusting for interest and tax, which are functions of changing, debt, and profitability, to give the new borrowings indicated.

117

Table 9.3

	1980	1981	1982	1983	1984	1985
	£m	£m	£m	£m	£m	£m
Base trading profits	7.1	8.6	10.1	11.2	12.2	13.3
Change in trading profit owing to sales change	(0.1)	(1.0)	(0.9)	(0.8)	(1.1)	(1.7)
Change owing to cost structure	(2.0)	(5.5)	(3.7)	(2.4)	(2.9)	(3.5)
Scenario trading profit	5.0	2.1	5.5	8.0	8.2	8.1

Table 9.4

	1980	1981	1982	1983	1984	1985
	£m	£m	£m	£m	£m	£m
Base working capital	13.9	15.0	15.8	17.5	19.3	21.2
Change in working capital owing to sales change	(0.2)	(1.8)	(1.5)	(1.2)	(1.8)	(2.7)
Change owing to working capital/sales movement	1.2	0.7	0.8	0.8	1.2	1.9
Scenario working capital	14.9	13.9	15.1	17.1	18.7	20.4

Table 9.5

	1980	1981	1982	1983	1984	1985
	£m	£m	£m	£m	£m	£m
Base trading cash flow	5.2	6.7	8.1	7.6	8.2	9.2
Change in trading profit	(2.1)	(6.5)	(4.6)	(3.1)	(4.0)	(5.2)
Change in working capital movement	(1.1)	2.1	(0.5)	(0.4)	0.2	0.3
Change in capital expenditure	0.0	0.0	0.1	0.2	0.2	0.3
Change in depreciation	(0.0)	(0.0)	(0.1)	(0.1)	(0.1)	(0.2)
Scenario trading cash flow	2.0	2.3	3.0	4.2	4.5	4.4

Table 9.6

	1980	1981	1982	1983	1984	1985
	£m	£m	£m	£m	£m	£m
Base total borrowings	9.2	5.6	2.6	0.0	(2.6)	(5.3)
Increase owing to scenario	3.2	6.0	8.9	9.5	11.6	14.9
Scenario/total borrowing	12.4	11.6	11.5	9.5	9.0	9.6

The disaggregation of the difference in financial variables owing to, say, volume changes, or movement in the working capital to sales or whatever, is not strictly necessary for producing the scenario. However, for analysis of the influences working their way through the system it can be very helpful indeed. The approximate causes of big changes can be seen quickly, and the planner can then back-track the effect through his models to develop the full story of the major influences. If the story has a basic credibility—the final hurdle is always the reasonable man test—then he can feel free to present it. In back-tracking he might find that the effect is due to a specific market suffering

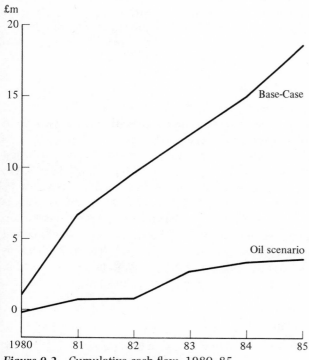

Figure 9.2   Cumulative cash flow, 1980–85

119

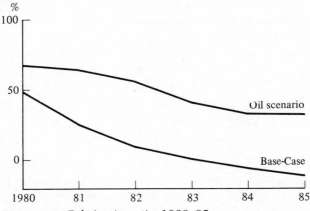

Figure 9.3 Debt/equity ratio, 1980–85

very severely. This in turn may be due to the micro-model specification, and it is as well to think through the chain of causation to ensure that no heavily biased assumptions have been made inadvertently. If they are present, they can be altered and the model re-run. A system made of separate building blocks as opposed to a monolithic mathematical edifice makes such checks and changes much easier and leaves the operator in control.

The relative cumulative cash flows are more immediately apparent from a graphical display (Fig. 9.2). And this results in a change in debt/equity ratio (Fig. 9.3).

Overall risk

In addition to risk shown by the foregoing, there is also that demonstrated in Chapter 7, arising from operational acceptability of the plans. The two uncertainties may be treated (with some caution) as additive to give the 'worst case' which represents the cash boundary within which plans will be laid. We say 'with some caution', because our scenario exercise should at best also be carried out on the revised results derived from the operational review of plans described in Chapter 7. In practice, it is possible to make a judgement upon whether the interaction between a revised business plan and different economic assumptions would be large. If it is not thought to be so, then it is as well to save the computing time and cost. A simple addition, as illustrated in Fig 9.4, gives a feel for the limits within which Conglom's plans may be laid.

Interpretation of scenarios

Even though the position does not appear too alarming overall, it could, nevertheless, be viewed by management as an unacceptable growth in

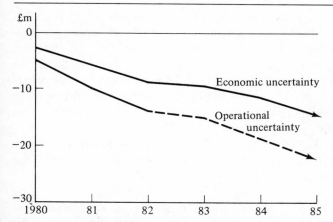

Figure 9.4 Cumulative cash flow compared with plan base-case

indebtedness, which, if it came about, would involve some drastic axe-wielding or forced sales to return to a short-term balance acceptable to creditors. Furthermore, in this case an executive who feared an even larger increase in the price of oil would have some sort of company benchmark to assess the significance of his petrophobia! Such actions might, however, do irreparable damage to longer-term prospects. It is, therefore, a question of deciding how probable this scenario is. If it were felt to be reasonably likely, some allowance, perhaps a full £10 million cash saving, would have to be made for the adverse economic environment. Plans would therefore have to be revised, perhaps stretched to span a longer period, such that if the environment turned as sour as the scenario suggests the corporation would still be able to carry out its revised plans in an orderly manner.

If the scenario were thought most unlikely to occur but others seemed credible, the management might take the worst of the remainder or some middle route through them. Since the amount of debt a company is prepared to take on is, typically, somewhat flexible, there remains quite a large discretionary area in terms of the extent to which plans should be revised. This may not always be the case. A company with a very high debt/equity ratio and nervous creditors may have very little flexibility and, therefore, be very cautious and feel obliged to consider making adjustments consistent with a low-probability scenario with a large impact.

The impact on strategies

Having decided the overall risk for which to make provision, there comes the more difficult task of specifying how individual activities are to be affected. The system described addresses the problems of the top management in a conglomerate, whose rôle is essentially that of a banker, albeit a highly interventionist one. Their concern is to ensure that the whole portfolio produces a good return on the funds invested and that the liabilities (borrowings) do not exceed an acceptable level. At any point in time each activity, if it is properly run, will have a suitable long-term market strategy that it is seeking to fulfil. When it prepares its plan for the medium term (say, five years), taking cognizance of the economic environment, it will make provision for the costs of executing that strategy.

Suppose that the aim of the medium-term strategy is to expand market share by acquisition; then somewhere in its plans a sum will be set aside for a specific take-over. On the other hand, most activities will have a simple, no change market strategy—that is, they will have the task of simply maintaining market share and focusing all attention on producing an efficient cost base. This may involve some capital expenditure, which will be reflected in the plans. In fact, it is tempting to suppose that, because a five-year plan is being drawn up, somehow something radical or new should be occurring in market strategy. In most cases this simply does not happen, because it is unnecessary.

Although a company should have a mechanism for generating new strategies and assessing their worth, it is most unlikely that major changes will be going on in all activities simultaneously. In fact, pursuing growth across a wide front can absorb an alarming quantity of cash and rarely represents a wise course for a conglomerate. Furthermore, the notion that corporations are always making decisions about large investments in plant that will take many years to build and yield profit over the decades is misconceived. These sorts of decisions do occur sometimes—more so in heavily capital-intensive industries—but they tend to be rare rather than frequent.

This excursion into strategies illustrates the point that activities within a portfolio will be pursuing individual market strategies, justified outside the scenario exercise, and rarely containing the big bank-bursting outlays. For these businesses, top management is concerned that the strategies can be pursued without overextending the company as a whole—that is, that they are capable of being carried out under all foreseeable circumstances. Perhaps even more important is their knowing what cash they will generate over the medium term under different economic circumstances. On this the larger decisions of major acquisitions may depend; what sort of resources might be available in the near future? The scenario system provides the necessary answer, though, of course in practice confirmation would always be sought from activity management.

Management action

Looking more specifically at Conglom's possible management response, the

122

assumption is that management does not want to remain exposed to the full impact of borrowing all the shortfall. A number of options are open to it:

- attack costs
- cut working capital
- postpone capital expenditure
- curtail growth
- dispose of an activity
- lower the dividend
- issue more shares

Some of the options are time-constrained. A rights issue can be done only at a suitable time according to the Stock Market—and in any event should be done only at a time advantageous to the corporation. Others may also have a timing element, in that they are appropriate on the downside but not the upside of the cycle. Disposal of an activity should, at best, be undertaken after the top of the cycle, when the best history can be shown.

Furthermore, in a well-managed operation, there should, in theory, be no room to make any of the cuts without affecting the longer-term position. Thus, a reduction in working capital or fixed capital expenditure may result in reduced service to the market place, perhaps lower quality of goods produced, and, in some cases, an inability to manufacture enough to follow a growth strategy. If there is an expectation of a bounce-back in demand in the near future, an overly stringent policy with receivables may result in loss of customers, either through ill-feeling, or even because they have been driven out of business.

Notwithstanding all these dilemmas of choice, however, management has to decide among the various options and carry out a particular policy and set of tactics. The set adopted will result from a trade-off between long-term strategy and the short-term needs of the business. So it makes the only sense to design these strategies in the light of business vulnerabilities, perceived by testing response to change in the environment.

Conglom's management, therefore, is now at the point where it makes its decisions, but we shall draw back at this point and avoid commitment on our own views. Perhaps the options may provide useful argument for business school case studies. We only seek to re-emphasize that, without undertaking the scenario exercise, the management could not assess adequately the risks being faced or how to measure them—and, in consequence, how to provide sufficiently for them by changing tactical direction. Other things could happen to Conglom worse than that exposed in our oil scenario. There might even be scenarios that point to a significant upside potential. While we have concentrated on downside risk, the system deals equally well with situations more optimistic than the plan.

Conglom is not at present in a particularly strong business position compared with others. It can predict no better what *will* happen, but its managers have explored the structure of the component activities, have considered the important features of the environment, and know how they will respond to events. When unexpected meteorites or battle fleets or magnetic storms appear on the radar screens of their space-ships, they won't scratch and yawn and say 'We'll have to get those screens fixed.' They will understand the bleeps and be ready to take action.

10.
The politics of planning

The acceptability of scenario planning

At a planning symposium for chief executives held in London recently, where about a dozen of the top blue-chip UK corporations were represented, the representative of the oil sector was commenting on his organization's use of scenario planning.

'Our planners have an international reputation. They've been doing this sort of thing now for a number of years and have persuaded our managers of the importance of their work by being right about many of the uncertainties.'

He went on to explain how this team had first crossed his path at a presentation overseas in the early 1970s, before the 1973 crisis; they had warned then of the likelihood of major oil price rises. They had been listened to politely, of course, but with little belief. Ten years on, their scenarios are viewed as an essential and integral part of the management process for the corporation.

'That's fine for you,' observed another from a more beleaguered industrial sector, 'but it doesn't seem relevant when you're fighting for survival. People get cynical about planning at a time like this.'

These two views represented the two ends of the spectrum of opinion at that meeting and, indeed, in the business world generally. To those steeped in planning methodologies, it is always a shock that people, even at the top of the commercial tree, can doubt the importance of techniques such as the use of scenarios. But responsibility for this situation must lie with the planners themselves. Any salesman in a high-technology area knows that it takes a long time and very careful nursing of the market to get a new product accepted. When the new product requires its users to adopt an attitudinal change, a change that requires a significant shift in the way of thinking about multi-business corporations, the process of adaptation is likely to be prolonged.

The planner, therefore, has to act like a salesman, using all the tricks of the trade to persuade and convince. The first and dominant requirement is a thorough and competent knowledge of the technology that is to be sold. At present, expertise in scenario planning tends to be found in pockets rather than generally. As we pointed out in Chapter 1, it is founded on comparatively new developments in computer-modelling techniques; it also requires the simultaneous coming together of the right disciplinary team. It will be some time, therefore, before there are enough scenario 'salesmen', with experience and expertise enough, to make a substantial impact upon management generally.

Planners need some winning cards

Our early efforts to achieve acceptance of the system within our own corporation seemed necessarily to be hampered by the fact that we were trying to develop the structure as we actually used it. In retrospect, this was perhaps not a bad card in the pack: it may have been an advantage, because earlier versions had a simplicity that now seems naive, but must have represented an easier introduction to our managers.

We had a number of other good cards, too. One of the most important was the continuous and interested support of the chief executive. There are still many corporations where some form of planning system exists only for cosmetic reasons, and not because top management believes in the plans or planning method. There is a semantic problem here, because we believe that planning must be devoted largely to the gathering, manipulation, and dissemination of information to enable decisions to be taken with the best information available. So even the most earthy manager must indulge in some planning. In the context of this paragraph, we are really talking about a formal and relatively structured system, which the chief executive uses not merely to acquire information, but also as a specific tool in the implementation process—for monitoring, controlling, stimulating change, and so on. In such a situation, it is clear that, without the support of the chief executive, the system cannot co-operate. Further, without his active use of it, it cannot be fully effective.

A second situation of which we were able to take advantage was the evidence around our managers that the problems facing them from an increasingly hostile environment would not go away without vigorous action. Planning has, in fact, tended to be fostered by businesses in difficulties or suddenly shaken by violent shock, where those in charge recognize that there have to be changes in the structure of the business and in the direction of its strategies. On the other hand, many highly successful operations run by entrepreneurs with flair (and luck) reject formal planning, because they have done very well without it. Leaving aside the nagging question of whether they might not have done even better with it, there must, nevertheless, surely come a day when the markets, the competitors, the suppliers, or even the managers themselves change. Reappraisals outside the scope of executive experience, even in these organizations, will demand a formal intelligence and decision-making system.

The third benefit we enjoyed was the gathering together of the right people at the right time who were able to construct the system effectively. Bill Bane, an engineer by training, with an unbelievable gift for getting to the core of structural design problems, was the architect of the system. Keith Roberts, one of the most brilliant mathematicians we have met, joined the team to build the strategic models and put the whole system together; Kin Huang, our accountant who built the financial models, was the other member of the original team. It was the conjoining at a high level of expertise of so many different disciplines that was, in the event, a key factor in our success.

The opposition

While we may have been particularly fortunate in having been dealt a good hand, it is clear that others will have a much tougher experience. There can be very strong opposition to the sort of approach outlined in this book. In fact, it is the general rule rather than the exception that planners who attempt to implement systems such as scenario planning are doing so in the face of a most hostile bureaucracy. The vested interests that are under attack are widespread and often powerful.

Where are these vested interests? Typically they occur in three areas:

- operating managers, who perceive, often quite rightly, that the searchlight of a properly structured system may reveal too much for their comfort.
- controllers—not necessarily the finance men—who are often very astute and flexible, but who have learned to run a business the old way and certainly do not want to change now.
- the highly paid, whose reward comes from being able to achieve success according to the old measures of performance.

In the 1960s planners, who were just beginning to emerge as a recognizable species, used to quote Machiavelli:

> There is nothing more difficult to take in hand, more perilous to conduct, or more uncertain in it's success, than to take the lead in the introduction of a new order of things, because the innovator has for enemies all those who have done well under the old conditions and lukewarm defenders in those who may do well under the new.
>
> *The Prince*

In the face of the antagonists described above, this remains just as true today.

Looking a little more closely at the three categories of opposition, it is clear that some managers are dismissive of planning because they do not want to tell all. Their opposition may well take the form of denying that it is possible to simulate the world, or at least their part of it, in a structured way. We have shown that this is not so. Of course it can be done, though in no way fully to replace human judgement.

But the alibi that it is impossible to foresee events won't hold water for much longer. Planning engineers can now improve upon their models, and they will gather more and more experience of the possible events for which the systems should provide. A large body of information, pointing up the consequences of such events, will become available. We shall still be unable to predict which particular shock is going to challenge us next, but we stand a reasonable chance of knowing what action to take if one does. So the manager

127

who asserts: 'But there was no way I could know this was going to happen' is quite right. Of course he couldn't! But if he then alleges that, in consequence, there was nothing he could do about it, this is the point where he gets fired. The least he could do is to consult his information system and consider what the contingency plan might be. At best, he may have already covered the eventuality by a scenario to develop a sufficiently robust strategy.

The second reason for opposition, that people who have worked in one way for a long time just do not want to change, is understandable—they go back for a time to square one, along with all the youngsters. And if their only hold on their status was experience in an outworn expertise, they may lose the race with those who are up-and-coming. We do not suggest that managers themselves will have to learn how to construct systems for scenario planning, any more than we would recommend they learn how to build printing presses or word-processors. They will, however, have to understand what such systems can do and which buttons to touch to get it done. If the operator of any machine doesn't understand it, he can only make very limited or random use of it, and in the end, it will grind to a halt, or race, or gibber at him; the benefit of using a machine will be lost—and the engineer is then likely to be castigated, too, for incompetence! The modern manager using a planning 'machine' is precisely in this position.

But why should the managers have to acquire this new skill themselves? Why not leave it to their professional planning advisers to run the system and interpret the information for them? The answer must be that, by adopting such a stand, the manager limits severely his personal opportunity to understand his business and its environment and, hence, to run his activity more successfully. There is no limit to learning, and this is an important educational aid. So we assert that the competent manager should have his own information console and alone, or surrounded by a bunch of assistants, should play with the data, get a better feel for the dynamics of his business, and see the best way through the commercial maze.

Perhaps another good reason for insisting on at least a partial D-I-Y approach is the need to avoid the emergence of a new, élitist priesthood. Even though we believe that our system may be honestly used by planners and that it is certainly a good deal more scientifically based than the inspired inspection of the tripes of sheep and geese, the principle is the same: possession of the information base, and the accepted means of interpreting it, gives the practitioner in such a favoured position a head start over his rivals in the power game. Planning must always remain in the hands of those nominated to make the decisions and be responsible for them; these executives must, therefore, participate in the manipulation of the information and must not abdicate responsibility in favour of a new priesthood.

There are, in fact, signs that managerial participation is already beginning to take place. Down in Texas, a consulting firm has installed a system in some of its client's offices which enables the corporate officers to sit round and play tunes on a wide variety of corporate data bases.[1] Maybe there's a bit of overkill in what has been done at one location, where the conference room table has a built-in console facing each chair. The executives could communicate with one another through the computer alone, without having to raise their eyes from the screen or speak a word. So why the curious old-fashioned idea of actually bringing people together in one room? There will, inevitably, be excesses in the way that enthusiastic pioneers adopt and adapt to the new opportunities—we would certainly deprecate any system that significantly reduced personal contact. There is no quicker way to kill corporate creativity. Nevertheless, the Texans (and others) are pointing in the right direction.

Over the past year we have been gathering information about the employee incentives applied by major corporations in the UK and USA to see how far they were directed towards the implementation of long-term goals. As already indicated, we found that, where there were incentive schemes in operation—which was rarer than we had expected, though we have still not got too far with our researches—most acted more as a stimulus to the maximization of short-term cash flow and short-term profit. In the UK, successive governmental interference in pay bargaining with squeezes and freezes appears to have killed stone dead the intelligent use of incentives for strategic purposes. The time is, however, now ripe for a reappraisal.

In the USA, there are one or two major corporations that have applied a sophisticated approach to the problem.[2] The concept is to weight incentives according to the strategies adopted by the business. Key tasks are divided into long-term, short-term, and timeless and according to whether the activity is to grow, maintain its market position, or be harvested, so the incentives are geared.

In general, however, the attitude tends to be to try to whip management up to achieve this year's targets rather than those of the next five years. The direction of post-Second World War industrial and commercial development up to the late 1960s undoubtedly engendered this attitute of 'get it right now and the future will take care of itself'. We now are learning, however, that, unless we take care of the longer-term future, it may never arrive for us at all. Not that we advocate relaxing on short-term targets. Scenario planning teaches us that, for most businesses, action now may be essential for the future. What is important is that, having surveyed the more distant horizon, the carrot or the goal will be applied to taking the most appropriate path to the ultimate destination, rather than the path that looks as though it will afford the quickest immediate progress, but ends in a cliff face round the corner.

Introducing scenario planning

Given a good system, a competent team, and an anticipation of no more than average opposition, how should a planning manager set about actually introducing the system to his organization? The reality is that it can never be imported wholesale, because a system has to be tailored over a period of time to fit the organization, rather than the other way round. Nevertheless, there are some ways of easing the process. We were entertained by the description given by one planning VIP of how he had persuaded his colleagues at corporate headquarters to adopt a new planning approach.

'I started by talking to the President informally about the ideas. He wasn't antagonistic, but didn't want to give his blessing then and there, so he suggested that I meet with him and a couple of his senior colleagues. There were three on his side of the table. I took along three of my people who really knew their stuff, so we had a majority. We asked for the help and suggestions of the bosses and they got hooked. At the next meeting of the President's Committee, these three plus myself and my deputy in attendance were again the majority, proposing and defending the new approach. And so on, right through to the Board. We were launched.'

'Mind you,' he added, reflectively, 'I seem to remember that when the new system was first discussed with me, I was the only one in the room who hadn't been working on it!'

Obviously this approach will not work unless the system to be introduced is both valid and useful, but given that, the planner has to recognize that it will not necessarily be accepted on its merits. He has to engineer its acceptance. Furthermore, he should not push others outside a very small circle into committing themselves to a belief in his methods. The most he needs or can expect is to get them to promote or use the system he believes in, whatever their motives may be. If the system is good, they will adopt it as their own in due course. They should not be asked to wear a button for it.

Once the system is launched, the next year or two are likely to be concerned with getting the data base straight. The planners have to maintain close contact with operating managers to improve the data content and avoid the yah-boo gibes of 'garbage in, garbage out'. The use of models can be educational in this context, but pointing to the implications of some of the wilder projections of margin, volumes, market share, and so on, but broadly this phase of introducing something like scenarios requires a gently nurturing approach.

At this time the outputs of the system also need to be published circumspectly. Over-simplification of the results rather than a rigorous intellectual honesty must be preferred. Indeed, it is probably true that this attitude must prevail at any period. The purpose of scenarios is to guide the decision-making process. Excessive detail obscures the issues. The uncertainty implicit has to be ignored at times. Even planners must make decisions!

At this stage of development, communication is as important as analysis. We made the decision, during the first year of introducing our systems, to

130

spend as much time and money on communications as on running the numbers through the computer. We admit, to, to some deliberate subterfuges —using a highly coloured, slick 35 mm presentation, when we sought to show the professionalism of our approach, rather scratchy overhead projector slides with typewritten messages when we wanted to get closer to the audience and achieve a dialogue, and so on. The objective was always to get people to use the systems first and reject them only afterwards, if they had to. In the event, education by infection rather than by didactics provided a successful route.

A question of lead times

Though the planner may have cleared all the hurdles mentioned in the foregoing and have implemented a satisfactory system, there are still a number of problems that he has to face. The first of these is the lead-time required for planning in a multi-business corporation. In the normal highly stratified corporation, the planning for a particular activity might occur within the framework of Table 10.1.

Table 10.1

Date	Event
July 1	Plan instructions from corporate HQ to divisions.
July 15	Plan instructions (modified) from division to activity.
Aug. 1	Activity manager instructs sales force, etc., on information requirement.
Aug. 15	Sales force, etc., provide reports to activity manager.
Sep. 1	Activity manager prepares activity plan and submits it to division.
Sep. 15	Divisional management discuss plan with activity manager and agree changes.
Oct. 1	Activity manager revises and resubmits.
Oct. 15	Division consolidates activity plans and submits to corporate HQ.
Nov. 1	Corporate management discuss plan with division and agree changes.
Nov. 15	Division re-discusses with activity, which agrees changes and resubmits activity plans.
Dec. 1	Division reconsolidates and resubmits plans to corporate HQ.
Dec. 15	Corporate management accepts plans and submits to board for ratification.

What a combersome series! Yet is inevitable where, first, information is locked into the personal files and memory stores of the managers on the shop floor and in the field and, second, communication may be effectively conducted only on pieces of paper or by word of mouth. It is inevitable, because the manager at divisional and corporate level cannot contain in his own mind all the data needed to maintain an adequate model of each activity structure, of each market or each micro-linkage, or of the macro-environment generally. He has to be reminded of the shape and direction of the curve for each business before he applies his mind to decision-making.

The problem that this long lead time then creates for scenario-planners is that, as pointed out in Chapter 6, the Base-Case assumptions are out of date by the time plans are agreed and a new simulation scenario has to be developed. There are, nevertheless, the means to circumvent this. The models, working from change to the Base Case, can themselves substitute for much of the personal files and memories, the pieces of paper, and the verbal descriptions. As we continually insist, we cannot do without human knowledge or expertise, but there is now a decreasing need to go though the whole *literate* process. The plan base-case assumptions can go into a data base to which all reporting activities would have access. According to the strategies, the activity manager can test on his own VDU proposals for increasing, maintaining, or reducing volume and/or price, and can consider this against cost movements. His proposals are then input and will be available on a further data base, accessible to him and to his immediately superior management. When any sets of activity proposals are accepted, these can be released up to the next hierarchy of management. Testing, modifying, and reworking can all be done in a matter of days, with managers of critical businesses in attendance as the real decisions are discussed, argued, and negotiated. And those whose contribution to planning in the past has been an eagle eye for accounting discrepancies will find themselves without a job.

The major benefit of such a system is that it will enable the planning game to be played in real time. No longer will assumptions be established in June for a plan that starts in January. The lead time will be drastically reduced, avoiding all the problems of having to take central provisions against changes in the environment. And the corporate economist may not have to revise his base-case scenario.

In fact, it will prove possible to move from once-a-year plans to a more flexible system—forecasts (and commitment) by managers will be made on whatever time-scale may be appropriate to the particular business. Thus, a longer business plan horizon would be suitable for the activity selling atomic power stations, compared with that in a consumer fashion business. The only danger is that such flexibility could get out of hand, and the relative simplicity of single annual profit and cash flow targets tucked into the chief executive's mind could become submerged under a welter of continuously changing data; he could lose his bearings and become a servant to his black boxes. Evolution, not revolution, will therefore be the only safe approach to such change.

Another unpopular aspect of planning, as viewed by the front-line troops, is the apparently excessive number of people engaged in it. Again, the fuller use of modern technology will reduce the numbers employed in the information-gathering routines. It is, however, neither feasible nor desirable to run short on the expertise needed to manipulate the information in a way that clarifies the problems for the high command and improves the intelligence available to the units in action. Inevitably, there will still be accusations that the staff are largely parasitical, even when the department has been pared down to its leanest. Such attitudes can be overcome only by the planners' maintaining close contact, being seen frequently in the front line, and trying to answer some of the questions posed by the troops, rather than staying in their cosy HQ billet and working solely for the C.-in-C. In the end, it is the personal relationship between planning and operating managers that will prove critical to adoption of any system.

The rôle of the planning director

This brings us finally to the rôle that the man in charge of the planning department has to play. One of the currently dispiriting ftatures about planning is the way in which, in some organizations, successive directors of this function treat it as a personal political football. There is an insistence on changing not only the emphasis, but also the whole structure of the corporate system. We certainly accept a mildly Maoist approach in that, as people move on, as the environment fluctuates, as new threats and opportunities arise, we have to adopt an attitude of constant evolution and throw out any bits of the models that have been superseded by something better. We must not become atrophied, and must not always try to solve new problems by outdated means. Once the general structure of a system, and, in particular, of the information base, has been established, however, it should be such as will enable new problems to be satisfactorily addressed. The information base may be augmented, but there should be no need to change it fundamentally. New techniques may be added, but neither PIMS nor policy directional matrices, nor experience curves, nor any other tool that is the particular pet of the director should dominate a corporation's planning system in the future. Planning managers will no longer make their mark by introducing some possibly significant new mechanism; they should not expect to revolutionize corporate thinking in this way, because they will only be producing information by a new route. Gradually, there will emerge a greater commonality in the systems in use by well-managed corporations. And then it will be possible for experts to move freely between these corporations: professionalism, as well as personality, will be the key to good planning.

Notes

1. The Interactive Financial Planning System, Execucom System Corporation.
2. General Electric is the particular example we have used.

Appendix 1.
Definitions

Sales
The invoiced value of goods and products sold over the period, excluding the amount of any value added tax or sales tax.

Raw materials
Raw materials include all bought-in materials and services directly incorporated in the product sold, excluding energy (see below).

Energy
All energy (including steam when applicable) directly consumed in production, but not produced by the activity.

Employment costs
Wages, salaries, employer pension contributions, and employer national insurance contributions. Excludes external recruitment and training costs and fringe benefits.

Central charges
The allocation of divisional headquarters' costs by each division to its component activities.

Extraordinary items
Unusual non-recurring profits or losses—e.g., profits or losses on divestment, sale of intestments or associates, major rationalization, or restructuring provisions.

Value added
The difference between the total sales value of goods sold and the cost of bought-in materials and services consumed in manufacturing those goods.

Activity/trading profit
Sales less all historic costs relating to the normal trading operations of the activity/reporting unit. Sales exclude associated company sales. Costs exclude extraordinary items, central charges and interest.

134

Activity/trading cash flow
The cash flow generated from normal trading activities including all movements on trading capital and excludes that arising from extraordinary items, central charges, interest, revaluations or exchange movements.

Divestment
Disposal of a company, business, investment, or major asset which is material and is not in the ordinary course of business.

Cash flow before financing
Trading cash flow less cost of acquisitions plus divestment proceeds.

Working capital
Value of inventories plus receivables (i.e., trade debtors—including group—VAT or sales tax, investment grants not received, and other items of a trading nature) less payables (i.e., trade creditors—including group—VAT or sales tax, and other items of a trading nature). Bills receivable are included in receivables.

Average
'Average' is the arithmetic mean of a number of period ends from the beginning to the end of the year—as a minimum:

(Value at end of first quarter + value at end of second quarter + value at end of third quarter + value at end of year) ÷ 4.

As preference: sum of values at 13 period-ends ÷ 13; as on option: sum of values at 52 week-ends ÷ 52.

Inventories
The aggregate level of inventories (or stocks) of raw materials, finished goods, and work in progress, valued on a first-in first-out basis (FIFO).

Working capital movements
Movement on working capital items excluding movements arising on the acquisition or divestment of subsidiaries.

Fixed assets at cost
The original cost or valuation of all fixed assets still in use, including those fully written off.

Depreciation
The charge made to the profit and loss account which reduces the cost of fixed assets to zero or a specified residual value over a predetermined period.

135

Depreciation HCA
The depreciation on assets valued at their historic cost.

Depreciation CCA
The depreciation on assets valued at their current cost.

Capital expenditure, or *Fixed capital expenditure*
Cash expenditure on fixed assets during the year.

Fixed assets NBA
Cost or valuation less accumulated depreciation of operating fixed assets.

Trading capital
Fixed assets at net book amount plus working capital.

Capital employed
Fixed assets at a net book amount, and net current assets, plus investments, and associates.

Gross capital employed
Capital employed plus goodwill.

Goodwill
The excess of the cost of shares of a subsidiary (or of the cost of a business) over the net book amount of the tangible assets at the date of acquisition (exchange rates, where applicable, at date of acquisition to prevail).

Appendix 2.
Program for HP97 to provide ratios referred to in Figure 2.1

The following is a description of the procedures required to calculate the ratios referred to in Fig. 2.1.

Step 1
Complete the inputs shown on Schedule 1. The numbers to the right of certain boxes in Schedule 3 correspond to the input numbers on Schedule 1.

Step 2
Load the program shown in Schedule 4 into the HP97 calculator. Start the program by pressing Key A and then enter the inputs on Schedule 1 sequentially; each amount is keyed in figures and key R/S is used to enter them into the program, e.g., key 120 350 (sales), press R/S, key 107 210 (cost of sales), press R/S, and so on.

Step 3
The calculator will manipulate the data as soon as the final amount (goodwill) has been entered. Retrieve the results by pressing the recall key with the appropriate store reference. Schedule 2 lists the recalls. Read these off and enter them onto Schedule 2. The numbers inside righthand corners of certain boxes in Schedule 3 correspond to the output numbers on Schedule 2.

Step 4
Fill the boxes on Schedule 3 by entering from Schedules 1 and 2 the appropriate information (numbers outside boxes reference information coming from Schedule 1 and those inside boxes, that from Schedule 2). This diagram is a form of flow chart and the functions performed ($+$, $-$, $\times$, $\div$) are shown to the left of each box. The completed diagram gives a snapshot of the business analysed at any given time.

Schedule 1

Name: Year:

Input	Item	Comment	Amount
1	Sales	Total external	
2	Cost of sales	Incl. overhead	
3	Stocks	Year end	
4	Debtors	Year end	
5	Creditors	Year end	
6	Fixed assets	Year end at cost	
7	Depreciation	Cumulative to year end	
8	Investment income	Interest, associates, etc.	
9	Interest	Payable only	
10	Taxation	Payable	
11	Investments	Incl. term loans, etc.	
12	Other	Residual B/S items If positive enter as negative	
13	Cash	Incl. short-term deposits	
14	Debt	Incl. overdrafts	
15	Goodwill		

Schedule 2

Outputs	Key	Item	Amount
1	RCL 2	Working capital	
2	RCL 3	Trading profit	
3	RCL 4	Trading capital	
4	RCL 6	Profit pre-tax	
5	RCL 7	Margin	
6	RCL 8	Capital intensity	
7	RCL 9	Tangible assets	
8	RCL A	Profit after tax	
9	RCL B	Net tangible assets	
10	RCL C	Total equity	
11	RCL D	Gearing	
12	RCL E P/S	ROE	
13	RCL 1	Fixed ass. NBA	
14	RCL 2	Working capital sales	
15	RCL 3	ROTC	
16	RCL 4	Net debt	
17	RCL 5	ROI	
18	RCL 6	D/E ratio	
19	RCL 7	Earnings/assets	

Schedule 3

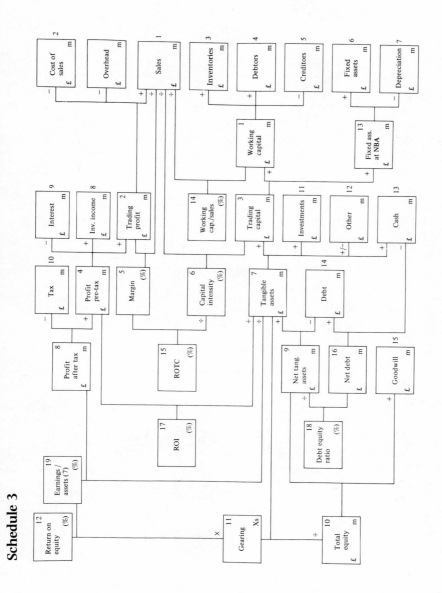

Schedule 4

Program Listing

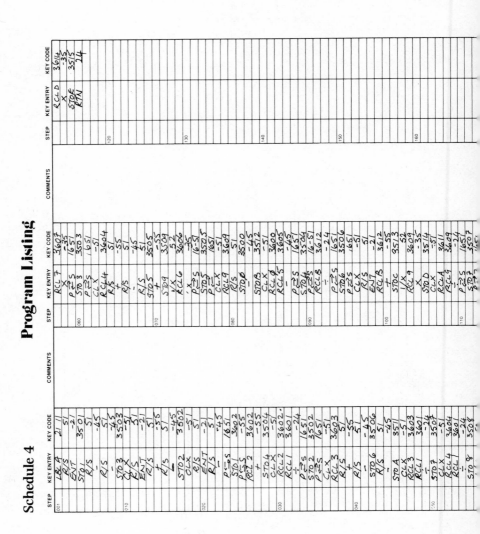

Appendix 3.
Conglom: Annual business plans, 1980–82

Schedule 1

Currency: £m

Date: 1 Nov. 79

Business plan, 1980–82: Conglom summary

		Actual			Original plan	Estimate as at period 8	Plan		
		1975	1976	1977	1978	1979	1979	1980	1981	1982
		(1)	(2)	(3)	(4)	(5)	(6)	(7)	(8)	(9)
Total external sales	(1)	35.0	49.4	55.5	58.2	66.5	66.8	75.7	83.5	89.7
Trading profit	(2)	1.6	4.3	5.0	2.7	4.8	5.2	7.1	8.6	10.1
Depreciation	(3)	0.8	0.8	1.0	1.2	1.5	1.2	1.6	1.8	2.2
Fixed-capital expenditure	(4)	1.2	1.0	2.5	3.2	2.9	2.7	3.1	2.6	3.4
Trading cash flow	(5)	1.0	3.7	1.2	(0.9)	2.7	2.1	5.2	6.7	8.1
Fixed assets NBA	(6)	9.4	10.0	11.5	13.5	14.9	15.0	16.5	17.3	18.5
Working capital	(7)	7.7	8.0	10.3	11.9	12.6	13.5	13.9	15.0	15.8
Trading capital	(8)	17.1	18.0	21.8	25.4	27.5	28.5	30.4	32.3	34.3
Ratios (%)										
Profit margin	(9)	5	9	9	5	7	8	9	10	11
Fixed-capital intensity	(10)	27	20	21	23	22	23	22	21	21
Working capital/sales	(11)	22	16	19	20	19	20	18	18	18
ROTC	(12)	9	24	23	11	17	18	23	27	29

Schedule 2

Currency: £m

Date: 1 Nov. 79

Business plan, 1980–82: Cash flow

		Actual		Original plan	Estimate as at period 8	Plan		
		1977	1978	1979	1979	1980	1981	1982
		(1)	(2)	(3)	(4)	(5)	(6)	(7)
Trading profit	(1)	5.0	2.7	4.8	5.2	7.1	8.6	10.1
Depreciation	(2)	1.0	1.2	1.5	1.2	1.6	1.8	2.2
Inflow from trading	(3)	6.0	3.9	6.3	6.4	8.7	10.4	12.3
Capital expenditure	(4)	2.5	3.2	2.9	2.7	3.1	2.6	3.4
Working capital movement	(5)	2.3	1.6	0.7	1.6	0.4	1.1	0.8
Trading cash flow	(6)	1.2	(0.9)	2.7	2.1	5.2	6.7	8.1
Net group interest	(7)	(1.0)	(1.2)	(2.0)	(1.8)	(1.1)	(0.4)	(0.1)
Dividends	(8)	(0.7)	(0.7)	(0.7)	(0.7)	(1.0)	(1.0)	(1.0)
Taxation (paid)/received	(9)	(1.1)	(0.3)	0.0	0.0	0.0	(1.7)	(4.0)
Total cash flow	(10)	(1.6)	(3.1)	0.0	(0.4)	3.1	3.6	3.0
Opening net long- and short-term borrowings	(11)	7.2	8.8	11.9	11.9	12.3	9.2	5.6
Movement on long-term borrowings	(12)	0.0	0.0	(0.8)	(0.8)	1.8	0.0	0.0
Movement on short-term borrowings	(13)	1.6	3.1	0.8	1.2	(4.9)	(3.6)	(3.0)
Closing net long- and short-term borrowings	(14)	8.8	11.9	11.9	12.3	9.2	5.6	2.6

Schedule 3

Currency: £m

Business plan, 1980–82: Balance sheet

Date: 1 Nov. 79

		Actual		Original plan	Estimate as at period 8	Plan		
		1977	1978	1979	1979	1980	1981	1982
		(1)	(2)	(3)	(4)	(5)	(6)	(7)
Fixed assets— closing NBA	(1)	11.5	13.5	14.9	15.0	16.5	17.3	18.5
Working capital	(2)	10.3	11.9	12.6	13.5	13.9	15.0	15.8
Trading capital	(3)	21.8	25.4	27.5	28.5	30.4	32.3	34.3
Goodwill	(4)	4.1	4.1	4.1	4.1	4.1	4.1	4.1
Gross cap. emp.	(5)	25.9	29.5	31.6	32.6	34.5	36.4	38.4
Net short-term borrowings	(6)	2.8	5.9	6.7	7.1	2.2	(1.4)	(4.4)
Long-term borrowings	(7)	6.0	6.0	5.2	5.2	7.0	7.0	7.0
Taxation	(8)	0.3	(1.0)	0.0	(0.1)	1.7	4.0	4.1
Share capital	(9)	6.0	6.0	6.0	6.0	6.0	6.0	6.0
Opening reserves	(10)	7.8	10.8	12.6	12.6	14.4	17.6	20.8
Retained profit	(11)	3.0	1.8	1.1	1.8	3.2	3.2	4.9
HCA financing	(12)	25.9	29.5	31.6	32.6	34.5	36.4	38.4
Debt	(13)	8.8	11.9	11.9	12.3	9.2	5.6	2.6
Equity	(14)	12.7	14.5	15.6	16.3	19.5	22.7	27.6
D/E ratio (%)	(15)	69	82	76	75	47	25	9

143

Schedule 4

Currency: £m

Date: 1 Nov. 79

Business plan, 1981–82: Sales and profits

		Actual 1977	Actual 1978	Original Plan 1979	Estimate as at period 8 1979	1980	Plan 1981	1982
		(1)	(2)	(3)	(4)	(5)	(6)	(7)
Total sales	(1)	56.1	58.8	67.1	67.5	76.6	84.4	90.7
Inter-group sales	(2)	(0.6)	(0.6)	(0.6)	(0.7)	(0.9)	(0.9)	(1.0)
Total external sales	(3)	55.5	58.2	66.5	66.8	75.7	83.5	89.7
Trading profit	(4)	5.0	2.7	4.8	5.2	7.1	8.6	10.1
Net interest	(5)	(1.0)	(1.2)	(2.0)	(1.8)	(1.1)	(0.4)	(0.1)
Profit before tax	(6)	4.0	1.5	2.8	3.4	6.0	8.2	10.0
Taxation	(7)	(0.3)	1.0	(1.0)	(0.9)	(1.8)	(4.0)	(4.1)
Profit after tax	(8)	3.7	2.5	1.8	2.5	4.2	4.2	5.9
Dividends	(9)	(0.7)	(0.7)	(0.7)	(0.7)	(1.0)	(1.0)	(1.0)
Retained profit	(10)	3.0	1.8	1.1	1.8	3.2	3.2	4.9

Schedule 5

Industrial Services Ltd. (£m)

	1975	Actual 1976	1977	1978	Original plan 1979	Latest estimate 1979	1980	Plan 1981	1982
Business parameters									
Total sales external to activity	11.1	13.9	14.8	16.5	19.2	20.1	24.0	27.2	30.2
Sales external to group	10.7	13.3	14.2	15.9	18.6	19.4	23.1	26.3	29.2
Activity profit	1.2	2.0	2.0	2.3	2.7	3.0	3.6	4.2	4.8
Activity cash flow	0.7	1.8	1.8	1.6	1.3	1.3	2.0	3.1	3.7
Average working capital	1.9	2.1	2.2	2.4	3.1	3.5	4.4	5.0	5.5
Average inventories	1.1	1.2	1.2	1.3	1.3	1.6	1.9	2.1	2.4
Fixed assets at cost	2.8	3.0	3.4	4.1	5.5	5.2	6.5	7.7	9.1
Fixed assets NBA	1.6	1.7	2.0	2.5	3.3	3.2	4.1	4.7	5.5
Depreciation HCA	0.1	0.1	0.2	0.3	0.4	0.3	0.4	0.6	0.7
Depreciation CCA	0.4	0.4	0.5	0.6	0.9	0.7	0.9	1.1	1.3
Fixed-capital expenditure	0.2	0.2	0.5	0.8	1.2	1.0	1.3	1.2	1.4
Employment costs	2.5	2.9	3.3	4.0	4.4	4.8	5.6	6.4	7.1
Energy costs	0.1	0.2	0.2	0.2	0.2	0.2	0.2	0.2	0.3
Raw materials costs	6.0	7.4	7.3	7.8	9.1	9.2	11.2	12.7	14.0
Other charges	1.2	1.3	1.8	1.9	2.4	2.6	3.0	3.1	3.3
Extraordinary items	0.0	0.0	0.0	0.0	0.0	0.0	0.0	0.0	0.0
Number of employees	700	686	671	671	671	671	657	657	660
Indices and ratios									
Volume index	75	85	84	90	98	96	100	104	108
ROTC	35.1%	53.6%	49.1%	46.1%	42.8%	44.3%	42.6%	43.3%	43.9%
Profit margin	11.1%	14.7%	13.8%	13.8%	14.1%	14.8%	15.1%	15.5%	16.0%
Working capital/sales	17.4%	15.4%	14.6%	14.7%	16.0%	17.6%	18.5%	18.5%	18.3%
Capacity utilization	76.1%	82.7%	86.0%	94.4%	97.2%	99.9%	101.6%	97.3%	95.0%

Schedule 6

Consumer Services Ltd (£m)

	1975	Actual 1976	1977	1978	Original plan 1979	Latest estimate 1979	1980	Plan 1981	1982
Business parameters									
Total sales external to activity	6.2	7.6	9.4	11.1	12.6	13.3	15.5	17.2	18.6
Sales external to group	6.2	7.6	9.4	11.1	12.6	13.3	15.5	17.2	18.6
Activity profit	0.3	0.9	1.5	1.6	1.5	1.9	2.0	2.3	2.5
Activity cash flow	0.3	0.9	1.4	1.5	0.9	0.8	1.3	2.0	2.5
Average working capital	0.4	0.5	0.7	0.8	0.8	1.4	1.4	1.6	1.6
Average inventories	0.3	0.3	0.4	0.5	0.5	0.6	0.6	0.7	0.7
Fixed assets at cost	0.6	0.6	0.7	0.9	1.5	1.5	2.4	2.7	3.0
Fixed assets NBA	0.3	0.3	0.4	0.5	1.0	1.0	1.7	1.8	1.9
Depreciation HCA	0.1	0.1	0.1	0.1	0.2	0.1	0.2	0.2	0.3
Depreciation CCA	M*	0.1	0.1	0.1	0.2	0.2	0.3	0.3	0.3
Fixed-capital expenditure	0.1	0.1	0.2	0.2	0.7	0.7	0.9	0.4	0.4
Employment costs	1.7	1.9	2.2	2.7	3.1	3.3	4.0	4.3	4.7
Energy costs	0.1	0.1	0.1	0.1	0.1	0.1	0.1	0.1	0.2
Raw materials costs	3.3	3.7	4.4	5.3	6.2	6.3	7.4	8.1	8.7
Other charges	0.7	0.9	1.1	1.3	1.5	1.6	1.8	2.2	2.2
Extraordinary items	0.0	0.0	0.0	0.0	0.0	0.0	0.0	0.0	0.0
Number of employees	455	462	471	489	515	515	515	515	516
Indices and ratios									
Volume index	77	80	88	97	103	102	100	99	99
ROTC	48.0%	114.0%	136.8%	130.7%	86.2%	77.8%	64.1%	68.5%	73.4%
Profit margin	5.5%	12.3%	15.9%	14.8%	12.0%	14.0%	12.8%	13.4%	13.6%
Working capital/sales	7.1%	6.8%	7.5%	7.2%	6.2%	10.4%	9.3%	9.3%	8.4%
Capacity utilization	M*	M*	M*	M*	M*	M*	M*	M*	M*

* M denotes data missing or omitted.

Schedule 7

Consumer Manufacturers BV (D. Fl. m)

	1975	Actual 1976	1977	1978	Original plan 1979	Latest estimate 1979	1980	Plan 1981	1982
Business parameters									
Total sales external									
to activity	21.2	23.0	23.7	25.2	30.2	32.1	35.4	39.6	43.5
Sales external to group	21.2	23.0	23.7	25.2	30.2	32.1	35.4	39.6	43.5
Activity profit	(0.7)	(0.9)	(1.8)	(4.8)	(1.5)	(1.4)	1.3	2.7	4.1
Activity cash flow	(2.7)	(0.7)	(5.2)	(14.0)	(2.4)	(1.0)	0.4	2.4	3.0
Average working capital	3.5	3.4	3.5	5.6	7.6	5.8	7.0	7.6	8.3
Average inventories	4.4	4.7	7.7	7.8	7.6	6.0	6.5	6.9	7.3
Fixed assets at cost	27.1	26.7	30.8	38.4	40.8	42.4	44.3	46.9	49.5
Fixed assets NBA	12.1	13.2	15.5	20.7	20.8	20.2	19.9	19.6	20.0
Depreciation HCA	2.0	2.1	1.7	2.1	2.4	2.2	2.4	2.5	2.7
Depreciation CCA	2.1	2.6	2.8	3.0	2.3	2.5	3.1	3.7	4.3
Fixed-capital expenditure	3.8	2.0	5.0	7.1	2.5	1.7	2.1	2.2	3.0
Employment costs	10.9	11.2	12.8	14.2	11.7	12.4	13.5	14.5	15.6
Energy costs	1.6	2.4	2.8	2.8	2.8	3.2	3.6	3.6	4.0
Raw materials costs	2.8	2.6	3.2	3.7	4.7	4.5	4.9	5.1	5.4
Other charges	4.6	5.6	5.0	7.2	10.1	11.2	9.7	11.2	11.7
Extraordinary items	0.0	0.0	0.0	2.1	0.0	0.0	0.0	0.0	0.0
Number of employees	522	504	528	552	426	420	414	414	414
Indices and ratios									
Volume index	73	75	80	91	94	99	100	102	103
ROTC	(4.2%)	(5.4%)	(9.7%)	(26.3%)	(5.3%)	(5.2%)	4.7%	10.0%	14.5%
Profit margin	(3.1%)	(3.9%)	(7.8%)	(27.5%)	(5.0%)	(4.2%)	3.6%	6.9%	9.4%
Working capital/sales	16.4%	14.8%	14.8%	22.1%	25.2%	18.0%	19.6%	19.2%	19.2%
Capacity utilization	88.0%	81.9%	97.2%	94.1%	100.0%	94.9%	100.0%	100.0%	100.0%

Schedule 8

Industrial Manufacturers Ltd (£m)

	1975	Actual 1976	1977	1978	Original plan 1979	Latest estimate 1979	1980	Plan 1981	1982
Business parameters									
Total sales external to activity	14.3	23.6	26.4	25.5	28.3	26.6	28.4	30.3	31.1
Sales external to group	14.3	23.6	26.4	25.5	28.3	26.6	28.4	30.3	31.1
Activity profit	0.2	1.6	1.9	0.4	1.0	0.6	1.2	1.4	1.8
Activity cash flow	0.2	1.7	(0.5)	(0.8)	1.1	0.2	1.9	1.0	1.2
Average working capital	5.7	5.6	7.7	8.7	8.3	8.8	7.9	8.2	8.4
Average inventories	7.0	8.0	10.2	11.2	10.6	11.4	10.2	10.5	10.8
Fixed assets at cost	8.8	9.1	9.8	10.4	10.8	11.0	11.4	11.9	12.7
Fixed assets NBA	5.3	5.2	5.6	5.7	5.8	6.0	6.0	6.1	6.4
Depreciation HCA	0.2	0.2	0.3	0.3	0.3	0.3	0.4	0.4	0.5
Depreciation CCA	0.4	0.5	0.5	0.6	0.7	0.7	0.8	0.9	0.9
Fixed-capital expenditure	0.2	0.3	0.6	0.5	0.4	0.6	0.4	0.5	0.8
Employment costs	4.2	5.2	6.1	6.8	7.2	7.8	8.3	8.6	9.2
Energy costs	1.4	2.0	2.4	2.5	2.7	2.9	3.2	3.7	4.1
Raw materials costs	5.3	8.8	9.8	9.9	11.0	10.4	11.0	11.8	12.3
Other charges	3.0	5.8	5.9	5.6	6.1	4.6	4.3	4.4	3.2
Extraordinary items	0.0	0.0	0.0	0.0	0.0	0.0	0.0	0.0	0.0
Number of employees	1396	1481	1478	1451	1410	1440	1400	1350	1350
Indices and ratios									
Volume index	84	120	122	108	110	103	100	97	94
ROTC	1.8%	14.8%	14.3%	2.8%	7.1%	4.1%	8.6%	9.8%	12.2%
Profit margin	1.4%	6.8%	7.2%	1.6%	3.5%	2.3%	4.2%	4.6%	5.8%
Working capital/sales	39.9%	23.7%	29.2%	34.1%	29.3%	33.1%	27.8%	27.1%	27.0%
Capacity utilization	64.0%	90.0%	92.0%	82.0%	93.0%	78.0%	76.0%	73.0%	71.0%

Appendix 4.
Regression techniques

Ordinary least squares

If a systematic relationship existed between two variables, Y and X, this would soon become apparent by plotting them as a scatter diagram (see Figs A4.1a and A4.1b). The points in A4.1a conform to a distinct shape, with the Y values rising with X. Furthermore, for a unit increase in X there seems to be a definable increase in Y. On the other hand, Fig. A4.1b appears shapeless, with no relationship between X and Y.

Casual observation of Fig. A4.1a suggests that a straight line through the plot points, stretching north-easterly from the origin, might reasonably approximate the relationship between Y and X. Figure A4.1c illustrates the result. The straight line has the equation $\hat{Y} = a + bX$, where $\hat{Y}$ is the estimate of Y, a is a constant given by the value of Y at the point of intersection with the vertical axis, and the coefficient b is given by the gradient of the line. The

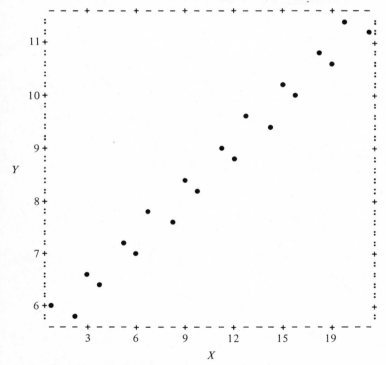

Figure A4.1a Scatter diagram with distinct shape: Y v. X

149

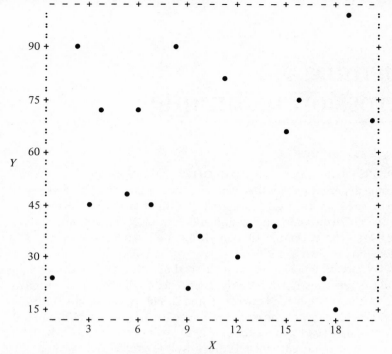

Figure A4.1b Scatter diagram without shape: Y v. X

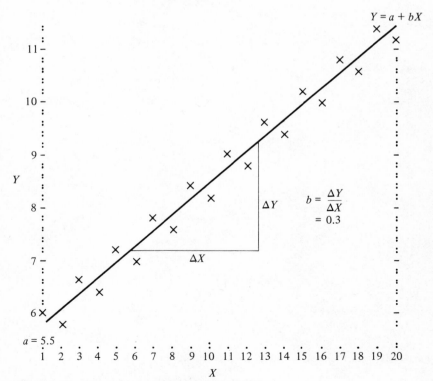

Figure A4.1c Drawing a line through the cluster

gradient or slope is derived by taking an increment in X (ΔX) and dividing it into the associated increment in Y (ΔY). In other words the approximation of the plot points by a staight line yields an equation that says that for a given value of X, there is a $5.5 + 0.3X$ value of $\hat{Y}$. This is the systematic part of the relationship. However, for any given value of X in Fig. A4.1C, Y deviates from the straight line, $\hat{Y}$. This difference is the random element.

What is needed, therefore, is a technique for fitting a line through the plotted data in such a way as to minimize the deviations. Furthermore, there is a need to know how well the fitted line approximates the data.

The line of best fit or regression equation, where there is one dependent variable and a single independent variable, is given by the simultaneous solution of these two normal equations:

$$\sum Y = Na + b\sum X \tag{A4.1}$$

$$\sum XY = a\sum X + b\sum X^2. \tag{A4.2}$$

Hence,
$$b = \frac{N\sum XY - \sum X \sum Y}{N\sum X^2 - \left(\sum X\right)^2} \tag{A4.3}$$

$$a = \left(\sum Y - b\sum X\right)N \tag{A4.4}$$

where Σ denotes the sum of items 1 to N. Effectively, it is seeking to ensure that:

1. the sum of all deviations add to zero (i.e., positive and negative deviations cancel);
2. the sum of the squared deviations is minimized.

Although the first requirement is obvious, it is not a sufficient condition for producing a line of best fit. In fact, any number of lines could meet the first requirement provided they passed through the co-ordinates given by the mean of X and Y. The second requirement is illustrated in Figs A4.2a and A4.2b.

The shaded areas respresent the square of the deviations between the actual value of Y and the one generated by the line of estimate, $\hat{Y}$. The line can be swung around through various positions (see Fig. A4.2a), but there will be only one point that minimizes the squares (see Fig. A4.2b). This is termed the principle of ordinary least squares, which is available on computer-based statistical systems.

The principle of ordinary least squares is not violated by the addition of extra-variables. In practice, most linkages will involve multivariate regression which is readily available on most computer statistical packages. The

151

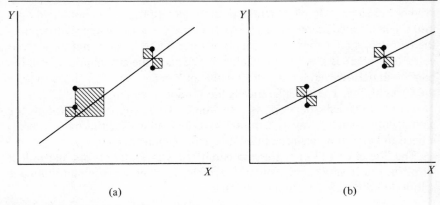

(a)   (b)

Figure A4.2   Principle of least squares

coefficients are interpreted in a straightforward manner, though their algebraic notation often causes confusion. For instance,

$$\hat{Y} = a_{1.23} + b_{12.3}X_2 + b_{13.2}X_3$$

is a familiar form of presentation. What does it all mean? The term $a_{1.23}$ is still the intercept and gives the hypothetical value of $\hat{Y}$, when X_2 and X_3 are both equal to zero. The coefficient $b_{12.3}$ indicates the amount by which a unit increase in explanatory variable X_2 will raise $\hat{Y}$, when X_3 is held constant. Similarly, $b_{13.2}$ gives the amount by which a unit increase in X_3 will raise $\hat{Y}$ when X_2 is kept constant. The number after the full point in the coefficient term indicates which variable is being held constant.

The notation underlines the important and useful feature of multiple regression. The coefficients are estimated on the basis of everthing specified in the equation being held constant. This allows one to specify models in terms of separate influences, which can then be measurably determined.

R^2 statistic

Having a line of best fit does not amount to having a line of good fit. It is helpful to have a measure of correlation between the independent and dependent variables. Above it was noted that the regression line would pass through the mean of the Y values, $\bar{Y}$. If the total variation in Y is given by:

$$\sum(Y - \bar{Y})^2 = \text{total variation.} \tag{A4.5}$$

Then the variation 'explained' by our estimate $\hat{Y}$ is:

$$\sum(\hat{Y} - \bar{Y})^2 = \text{explained variation} \tag{A4.6}$$

and the 'unexplained' variation is given by:

$$\sum(Y - \hat{Y})^2 = \text{unexplained variation.} \tag{A4.7}$$

Thus

$$\sum(Y - \overline{Y})^2 = \sum(\hat{Y} - \overline{Y})^2 + \sum(Y - \hat{Y})^2. \qquad \text{(A4.8)}$$

if the explained variation were expressed as a ratio of the total variation it would give the proportion of the total variation in Y that is explained by the regression line; this is called the coefficient of determination, but more popularly known as 'R-squared':

$$R^2 = \frac{\sum(\hat{Y} - \overline{Y})^2}{\sum(Y - \overline{Y})^2}. \qquad \text{(A4.9)}$$

If the unexplained element took a value of zero, it would imply that the regression line fitted perfectly and that the explained variation equalled the total variation. Under these circumstances R^2 would take a maximum value of one. By a similar piece of logic R^2 takes a minimum value of zero when the explained variation is zero. Thus, the closer R^2 is to one, the closer the plot points cluster around the regression line and the better the equation approximates the movement in the dependent variable. However, an R^2 close to zero need not mean that X and Y are unrelated; they may be related in a nonlinear fashion. Some indication of this is given by drawing a scatter diagram of the residual between Y and $\hat{Y}$ against the corresponding values of X. If the cluster appears to indicate a 'curved' shape, then it is worth linearly transforming the data and trying the regression again. On the other hand, even if $R^2 = 1$ the relationship may be spurious. Storks overflying Germany might be highly correlated with births in that country, but whatever the R^2, nobody is going to abandon traditional views on reproduction. This merely serves to underline the importance of starting with a plausible theory.

The coefficient of determination, R^2, is very helpful in telling the user that there is no relationship or that X and Y are perfectly related, but at what level of R^2 does one accept a regression equation? Unfortunately, there is no hard and fast rule, although when R^2 is below 0.5 it means that other, perhaps entirely random, factors explain more of the variation in Y than those postulated. In fact, Kane quotes an example of a consumption function published by Ando and Modigliani which had an $R^2 = 0.997$ which certainly testifies to its analytic validity.[1] However, if allowance were made for the inherent variability of the error term, it was shown that the expected errors were very large in relation to the annual changes in consumption. Thus the predictive power of the equation is not very great despite a 0.997 R^2. The point is that there is no single test factor that can suggest acceptance or rejection of an equation produced by least squares. All the same, there are very many tests available that can be useful in forming judgements.

[1] E. J. Kane, *Economic Statistics and Econometrics*, Harper & Row, New York, 1968.

Making inferences about the real world

Earlier it was suggested that data used to test an hypothesis about real-world relationships would necessarily be a sample, and there was some possibility that the regression would yield point estimates of the coefficients that were biased and had arisen by chance. Since the object of the exercise is to learn something about the real world, one needs to know what the confidence intervals are on the coefficients produced by least squares. Thus it might be possible to say there is a 0.95 probability that the real-world coefficient β lies within $b + s$, where b is the point estimate and s the margin of error. To do this it is necessary to know the probability distribution of the real-world error term U:

$$Y = \alpha + \beta X + U. \tag{A4.10}$$

Since this is unknowable, statisticians assume that the error term is a result of numerous independent disturbances, which therefore allows them to apply the law of large numbers. Specifically, they assume that the real-world error term is normally distributed. In fact, use is made of a normal probability density function which is shown in Fig. A4.3. This bell-shaped figure can be interpreted in the following manner. The area under the curve is the sum of probabilities of all possible values of U taking a value of one and mean value of zero. Suppose one wanted to know what was the probability of a certain value U lying between the intervals U_1 and U_2. The normal probability density function tells us that it is equal to the shaded area under the curve. Because the function is continuous, as opposed to discrete, it only makes sense to talk in terms of intervals since the probability of U taking a unique value is zero.

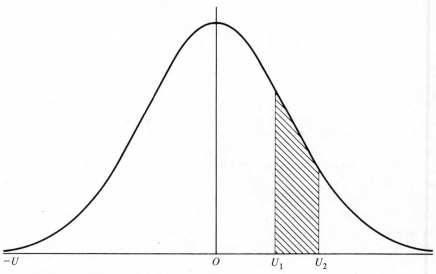

Figure A4.3   Normal probability density function

However, for an infinitesimally small range, there would be a non-zero probability of U lying between it.

The shape of the curve can be given by a quite complex equation, but all that need concern us is that its shape is determined by the mean (assumed zero) and the variance (dispersion from the mean), which is unknown. In terms of the real-world postulated relationship, $Y = \alpha + \beta X + U$, statisticians have the schematic view shown in Fig. A4.4. This three-dimensional view has the normal X, Y relationships. However, for each of these there is the third dimension given by the normal probability density function given by $f(U)$. It sits like a bell-shaped ridge centred over the postulated relationship given by $Y = \alpha + \beta X$. The real-world random term may lie within a given range of the dotted line. The proability that it falls within a given range is now determined by the volume under the ridge. The total volume, i.e., the sum of probabilities, is one; however, the shape of the ridge—narrow and high, or broad and low—is still determined by the variance, which is unkown.

Statisticians, not having knowledge about the real-world variance, take

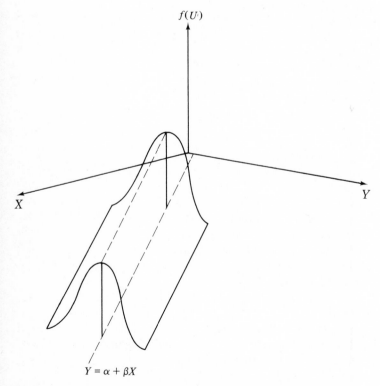

Figure A4.4 The variance of U in a regression model

155

the sample variance to get their normal probability density function. This can be derived by:

$$S_{YX}^2 = \sum_{i=1}^{N} \frac{(Y_i - \hat{Y}_i)^2}{N-2}.$$ (A4.11)

The positive square root of S_{YX}^2 is called the standard error of estimate, S_{YX}, and is normally given by all computer packages since it is a crucial statistic. It can be used in a variety of ways to tell the user more about the quality of the relationship.

Placing confidence internals of β

The postulated real-world relationship, $Y = \alpha + \beta X + U$, could be tested in a large number of different samples that would yield a variety of b coefficient estimates. The distribution of their values would conform to the 't-distribution' with the mean value of b equalling β. The t-distribution is a variant of the normal probability distribution, which, as far as the user is concerned, is displayed in the back of most statistics textbooks (see Fig. A4.5).

Selected confidence levels or probability values are set as column headings in Table A4.1. For a 0.95 probability or 95 per cent confidence level one would

Table A4.1 t-distribution tables: confidence levels

df	0.1	0.05	0.025	0.010
2			4.303	
:				
25			2.060	

go to the column '0.025' $(1-2(0.025) = 0{\cdot}95)$ and then track down the column to the row corresponding to the number of degrees of freedom (df) in the equation. This latter concept need not detain us except to note that its numerical value in this case is a function of the number of observations of the X variable (N) and the number of explanatory variables, k. Thus the degree of freedom (df) for a t-test is given by

$$df = N - k - 1.$$ (A4.12)

In the example so far there is only one explanatory variable, X. However, with multiple regression there should be more, so k would not equal 1 but 2 or more. At the point of intercept between the confidence limit, 0.025, say, and the df, 25, there lies the appropriate t-statistic, 2.060.

Confidence intervals are then calculated using:

156

$$\beta = b \pm \frac{t \cdot S_{\text{YX}}}{\sqrt{[\sum (X - \bar{X})^2}}. \qquad (A4.13)$$

The standard error of estimate appears in this somewhat complex equation. Fortunately, most computer-based systems provide the standard error of b:

$$S_b = \frac{S_{\text{YX}}}{[\sum (X - \bar{X})]^2} \qquad (A4.14)$$

so that the confidence intervals can be found quite simply:

$$\beta = b \pm tc\, df\,(S_b). \qquad (A4.15)$$

β thus falls within a range determined by the product of the t value (at c confidence level with df degrees of freedom) and the standard error of b, S_b. Suppose that the results of an ordinary least squares calculation involving one explanatory variable X with 27 observations produced the following results:

$$b = 0.75 \qquad S_b = 0.05.$$

The degrees of freedom would be $27 - 1 - 1 = 25$, and at the 95 per cent confidence level, c, the t-value is 2.06. So the confidence intervals would be:

$$\beta = 0.75 \pm (2.06)\,(0.05) = 0.75 \pm (0.103)$$

$$0.647 \leqslant \beta \leqslant 0.853.$$

From this analysis it is inferred that the real world β lies, with a 0.95 probability, between 0.647 and 0.853. Besides drawing attention to the fact that the real world may not conform to the six decimal places on the computer print-out, this test serves another important function.

Earlier, much was made of the requirement of starting with a testable hypothesis about the real world, and one of the crucial elements that needs to be specified prior to the regression is the expected sign on the various β coefficients. Indeed, in some circumstances the hypothesis might actually involve a β value falling close to a specific value. If a β value were to have the following confidence intervals, different interpretation could be placed on the regression equation:

$$-0.04 \leqslant \beta \leqslant 0.06.$$

The β coefficient could be either negative or positive, or indeed even zero. Thus an increment in X might either reduce Y, increase it, or leave it unchanged. If theory had required that β be positive, then this equation would have to be rejected since it could have a negative value.

It is intuitively obvious that, if $\beta = 0$, there is no relationship between Y and X. Most computer-based systems provide readily interpretable information to check whether β is significantly different from zero. To test the hypothesis that $\beta = 0$, the t-value is calculated:

$$t_{(calc)} = \frac{b - \beta}{S_b} \qquad (A4.16)$$

157

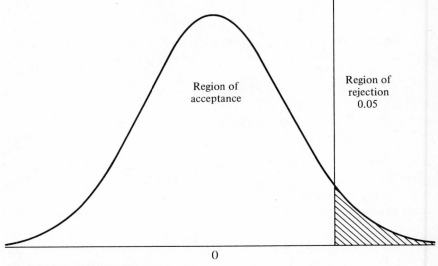

Figure A4.5 t-distribution

where β is set equal to 0. The calculated t-value is then compared with the value in the tables corresponding to the chosen confidence level and the degrees of freedom (df) (see Fig. A4.5). The test is set in such a way that one is testing for the condition that there is, say, a 0.95 chance that $\beta=0$ and so one is interested in the 0.05 value of t. If the $t_{(calc)}$ is greater than $t_{0.05}$, then the hypothesis that $\beta=0$ is rejected and the alternative hypothesis, say, $B>0$ is accepted. Using the previous example, where

$$b = 0.75 \qquad S_b = 0.05,$$

$$t_{(calc)} = \frac{0.75-0}{0.05} = 15.0$$

and since $t_{0.05}$ and $25df = 2.06$ one can reject the notion that $\beta=0$. Indeed, it follows that the higher $t_{(calc)}$ becomes relative to the $t_c=df$, the narrower becomes the confidence interval. In this case a glance at the $t_{(calc)}$ given by most computers would suggest that the variable associated with b is highly significant. This is equally true of multiple regression where there is more than one explanatory variable.

Where it is occasionally necessary to make tests on α, the confidence interval is given by

$$\alpha = a \pm t_c df(S_a) \qquad (A4.17)$$

where

$$S_a = S_{YX}\sqrt{\left\{\frac{\sum X^2}{N\sum(X-\bar{X})^2}\right\}}$$

and is normally given in most computer programs. The test for $\alpha=0$ is:

$$t_{(calc)} = \frac{a-\alpha}{S_a}. \tag{A4.18}$$

The above tests and confidence intervals depend on individual values of the error term U being independent of the values of each X and other U's in the sample. Futhermore, it is assumed that they follow a normal distribution with zero mean and a constant finite variance. This last condition, in terms of Fig. A4.4, means that the ridge does not have a tendency to fan in and out along its base. A little further on, tests are suggested to verify that the sample variance conforms to this assumption. If it does not, the variance is said to be heteroscedastic, and both confidence intervals and $t_{(calc)}$ will be distorted. Thus, even when confidence intervals have been estimated, it is not necessarily the end of the trail of tests. There remains a need to test the assumptions upon which they are based.

F-statistics and analysis of variance

Another test that frequently appears in statistical computer packages is the F-statistic and the analysis of variance. Earlier it was suggested that, if $\beta=0$, then X and Y were not statistically related, and a test was devised, $t_{(calc)}$, to establish from the sample b whether or not the real-world β was significantly different from zero. In multiple regression, i.e.,

$$Y = \alpha + \beta_1 X_1 + \beta_2 X_2 \ldots + \beta_n X_n + U, \tag{A4.19}$$

the F-statistic is used to test the hypothesis that $\beta_1 = \beta_2 = \beta_n = 0$.

As such, it represents a test of the whole equation. The F-statistic is calculated from the components of the analysis of variance table, which is occasionally reproduced in computer-based statistical packages, and makes

Table: A4.2 Analysis of variance table

Source of variation	Degrees of freedom	Sum of squares	Mean square
Explained	k	$\sum(\hat{Y}-\bar{Y})^2$	$\sum(\hat{Y}-\bar{Y})^2/k$
Unexplained	$N-k-1$	$\sum(Y-\hat{Y})^2$	$\sum(Y-\hat{Y})^2/N-k-1$
Total	$N-1$	$\sum(Y-\bar{Y})^2$	

use of the concepts of explained and unexplained variation (Table A4.2). The F-statistic is the ratio of the mean squares:

$$F = \frac{\sum\hat{Y}-\bar{Y})^2}{\sum(Y-\hat{Y})^2} \cdot \frac{N-k-i}{k} \tag{A4.20}$$

159

where N is the number of observations and k is given by number of explanatory variables.

The distribution of the F-statistic is normally given at the back of most statistics books, and all the user has to do is check the calculated values against these in the table at, say, the 5 per cent level. Both the row and column headings relate to the degrees of freedom. The column headings are the degrees of freedom k associated with the explained variation; the row headings are the degrees of freedom associated with the unexplained variation $N-k-1$ (see Table A4.3 for selected values). If the calculated F-statistic of a regression with 13 observations and 2 explanatory variables exceeded 4.26, then the hypothesis that $\beta_1 = \beta_2 = 0$ could be rejected. The result would be significant at the 95 per cent level. This is a convenient point to stress that adding variables to this equation will consume degrees of freedom which will push up the R^2 but set ever-higher hurdles for the F statistic and t-test.

Although there are many other tests, and they can be found in econometric text books, the R^2, t-test, and F-statistic provide sufficient insight. As has been shown, they are all derived from the standard error of estimate S_{yx} which is a

Table A4.3   Five per cent points of F-distribution

$f1$	$=$	1	2	3	∞
$f2$	$=1$				
	2				
	3				
	$\vdots$			5.41	
	5				
	$\vdots$				
	10		4.26		

function of the unexplained variation. The greater the R^2, the more of the variation in Y that is explained by independent X variables, and the larger is the systemmatic element in the sample. The sample is not the real world—indeed, it is sometimes dangerous to assume that it is, since it can lead to a set of regression permutations being performed simply to push up the R^2. It is conceivable that the random element is quite large. If this is true, then one must graciously accept and take heart that we are not all automatons. However, if the F-statistic and the individual t-statistics show high values relative to their test value, then the regression equation may prove acceptable for scenario planning. After all, the scenario-planner is seeking to establish what will happen as a consequence of an external shock. His models seek to demonstrate the systematic elements and, so long as these have been well identified, he will have a tool of some worth. It may not, however, be sufficient for forecasting.

160

A thorough approach to formulating equations requires that the assumptions underlying inference about the real world are also tested. In practice, there are two key assumptions which might be tested:

- non-autocorrelation
- homoscedasticity

With time-series analysis the assumption of non-autocorrelation is perhaps the more suspect of the two. Fortunately, violation of the homoscedasticity assumption is not as common with time-series as it is with cross-sectional regression. So what are these two assumptions?

Autocorrelation
Implicit in many of the tests and in the calculation of confidence intervals is the assumption that error terms in the real world are distributed independently of each other; that is, the value of one error term (e_t) is independent of the value of a previous error term. If autocorrelation is present, for instance if e_t is a positive function of e_{t-1}, it results in a biased estimate of the real-world variance that is derived from the sample variance. With positive autocorrelation one is likely to underestimate the real-world variance and perhaps reject the hypothesis $\beta = 0$ when one should not.

Figures A4.6(a) and A4.6(b) show a situation of positive first-order correlation. As with previous other diagrams, one can determine a 'shape' to

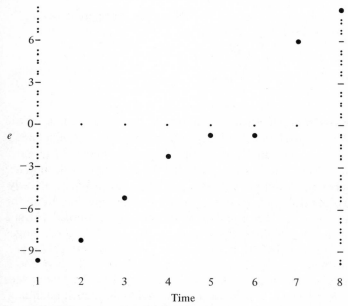

Figure A4.6a Errors plotted against time

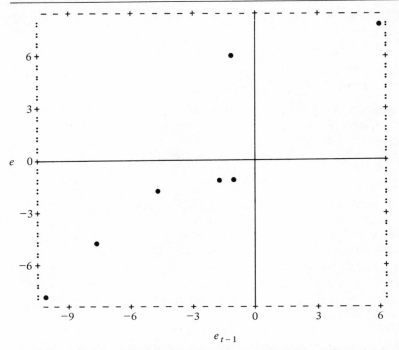

Figure A4.6b Scatter diagram showing positive first-order autocorrelation: e v. e_{t-1}

the cluster. It is normal to test for first-order autocorrelation using the Durbin–Watson statistic, d:

$$d = \frac{\displaystyle\sum_{t=2}^{n}(e_t - e_{t-1})^2}{\displaystyle\sum_{t=1}^{n}e_t^2}. \tag{A4.21}$$

The range of d spans from 0 to 4 with a midpoint of 2. The test is made on the hypothesis of no autocorrelation, and, depending on where the calculated d falls on the range 0–4, one can draw certain conclusions about the absence of autocorrelation. There are certain critical ranges within 0–4 that are established by upper and lower values of d, noted here as d_u and d_l respectively. Values of d_u and d_l are derived from the appropriate tables and depend on the number of explanatory variables, k, and the number of observations, N. Armed with these upper and lower values, it is possible to calculate the critical ranges and see where the calculated d falls. Table A4.4 summarizes the critical ranges.

If the Durbin–Watson statistic takes a value of close to 2, then one is normally safe in assuming no first-order autocorrelation. However, what does one do if it is present ? The first step is to test the residuals against additional explanatory variables, because it is quite conceivable that the detected

162

Table A4.4

Critical range	If calculated d falls in this range
0 to d_l	indicates probability of positive autocorrelation
d_l to d_u	cannot be sure if autocorrelation present
d_u to $(4-d_u)$	no autocorrelation
$(d-d_u)$ to $(4-d_l)$	cannot be sure if autocorrelation present
$(4-d_l)$ to 4	indicates probability of negative autocorrelation

systematic chatacteristics of the error terms are due to an omitted variable. Only when exhaustive testing has shown the autocorrelation cannot be removed by inclusion of other variables should it be accepted that the error structure is time-dependent and that the data must be transformed to take specific account of it. Techniques for doing this are normally on computer packages, e.g., Cochrane–Orcutt or Hildreth–Lu. These methods calculate a value rho (ρ) which transforms the fitted equation to the following form:

$$Y_{t-\rho}Y_{t-1} = a(1-\rho)+b(X_{t-\rho}X_{t-1})+e_t. \qquad (A4.22)$$

Homoscedasticity
In Fig. A4.4 the 'ridge' has parallel baselines, reflecting the assumption that each error term has the same variance (dispersion from the mean) and is

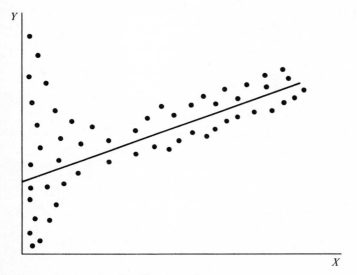

Figure A4.7   Example of heteroscedasticity

independent of the explanatory variable, X. Since the sample variance is used by assumption as if it were the real-world variance, the latter should be tested for a constant variance. If it is not constant, then the various tests to discover whether $\beta=0$ would be distorted. Like the presence of autocorrelation, it does not mean the estimate b is biased, but only that our view of β is not so narrowly circumscribed.

With only one explanatory variable, violation of the homoscedasticity assumption can be seen simply by plotting the data and the regression line. Figure A4.7 shows a situation where the variance of the error is greatest at lower values of X. There could also be circumstances where the variance increased with values of X. With multiple correlation, plotting data is not very helpful. However, one could test whether the variance has a tendency to be related to any of the X values using Spearman's rank correlation.

$$r_s = 1 - \frac{6\sum D^2}{N(N^2-1)} \tag{A4.23}$$

where d is the difference between the ranked order of the X values and the errors. Table A4.5 illustrates this. Spearman's rank correlation coefficient, r_s, takes values from $+1$ to -1. Zero values suggest no relationship in the order, while $+1$ indicates that the two rankings accord perfectly, high with high, low with low. An r_s of -1 means that rankings are perfectly but inversely related, high with low and vice versa.

Fortunately, heteroscedasticity does not occur often in time-series, since transforming the data to cope with the problem, especially in multiple regression, is no easy matter. Some techniques are mentioned in the literature mainly for bivariate regression, which normally requires prior correction for

Table A4.5

Period	Rank X_t	E_t	Values D	D^2
60	2	3	-1	1
61	4	4	0	0
62	1	2	-1	1
63	3	1	2	4
64	5	6	-1	1
65	6	7	1	1
				8

$$r_s = 1 - \frac{6(8)}{6(36-1)} = 0.77$$

any autocorrelation. All the same, it is preferable to know that one's regression is heteroscedastic when it is being interpreted than to remain in ignorance.

Multicollinearity

There is one final problem area that should be discussed, that is multicollinearity. So far, bivariate examples have been given, for simplicity of exposition; this has permitted the development of various concepts that have equal validity for multivariate regression analysis. There is, though, a special danger that arises from multiple regression, particularly with economic and market data. It is quite conceivable that the explanatory variables are closely related to each other, and therefore the estimating techniques discussed above cannot adequately sort out the individual contribution of each X to values of Y. Testing for multicollinearity in pairwise fashion is done simply enough by determining their r^2. However, that will not uncover the more subtle forms of multicollinearity. It is conceivable that X_3 is correlated with certain combinations of X_1 and X_2.

The consequences of multicollinearity for a model can be severe. The slope estimates may change radically as a result of a minor change in the data sample or model specification. Quite often one might be confronted with a situation of a very high r^2 where the t-values are not significant. This arises from the standard errors of the coefficients being characteristically high. Can anything be done to cope with this problem?

The solutions depend very much on circumstance. The collinear variables might be pooled in some way, perhaps by addition. Alternatively, if two variables genuinely function as one in the equation, perhaps one could be dropped. A third possibility is to take first differences of the series, either of their natural values or their logarithmic equivalent. Finally, if one is very confident that the relationship between the collinear variables is externally stable, then one could opt to use the equation despite the collinearity. However, because a quite small change in their relationship could result in a large change in the slope-estimate, caution is counselled.

Index